Sparks

THE
DISRUPTION
OF THE
SOLID SOUTH

THE
DISRUPTION
OF THE
SOLID SOUTH

GEORGE BROWN TINDALL

MERCER UNIVERSITY LAMAR
MEMORIAL LECTURES, NO. 14

UNIVERSITY OF GEORGIA PRESS

ATHENS

To my grandmother
Lucy Mercer Brown
and to the memory of
my grandfather
George Washington Brown

Contents

Foreword

ALMOST TEN YEARS SEPARATE GEORGE TINDALL'S *The Disruption of the Solid South* from Dewey Grantham's *The Democratic South*, but no two books in the Mercer University's Eugenia Dorothy Blount Memorial Lectures series fit so well as companion volumes. One other book in this series deals with the theme of politics in the South. It is T. Harry Williams' *Romance and Realism in Southern Politics*. For the student who wishes to understand southern politics all three of these books will be enlightening. Tindall's volume has an advantage in that it comes after about a decade of change since the publication of Grantham's volume, a period so pregnant with change that where Grantham could only see a trend Tindall sees a fulfillment. Thus *The Disruption of the Solid South* is an excellent sequel to the Grantham volume.

Professor George Brown Tindall, a product of and a teacher at the University of North Carolina, is a native of South Carolina. He is now Kenan professor of history at Chapel Hill. His craft has been perfected in teaching experience at universities in Louisiana, Mississippi, and Kentucky, as Fulbright lecturer at the University of Vienna in Austria, and in research and writing in southern history which has resulted in the production of prize-winning books such as *South Carolina Negroes, 1877–1900* and *The Emergence of the New South, 1913–1945*, the tenth volume in the *History of the South* series.

One chapter title underwent a change between the time of the lectures and the final preparation of the manuscript. Those who heard the original lectures will remember the third lecture was titled "Southern Strategy and the Volatile South." Beyond this the essays, as Professor Tindall states, have been altered only slightly in style. The substance is the same. The lectures were given at the time of the elections of 1970, and as they dealt with southern strategy from Hayes to Nixon they were most timely but held a risk for the historian who was trying to analyze and draw conclusions in a sort of on-the-spot situation. The historian's training kept him in proper perspective, however, and, as he says, the "returns and subsequent events have served more to confirm than to undermine the conclusions already reached."

Running through the entire period of change is the constant and ever visible thread of race. Nothing affected the party struggle in the South, and the political battle for control of the South, more than this central theme of southern politics. Williams dealt with it, naturally, and Grantham traced it as far as was possible in 1962. Now Tindall retraces the story from Reconstruction days and continues it to the present, giving the student a perspective which will help him better understand the significant events which have recently occurred in the region—and understanding them he can chart his future more wisely.

Mrs. Walter D. Lamar who made possible these lectures in southern history and literature was the daughter of James Henderson Blount, who represented his Georgia district in Congress from 1873 to 1893. She spent her life in dedicated service to her community and to her Southland. Much of the political struggle in and over the South described in this volume was a part of Mrs. Lamar's life, experienced through her father. She observed the political drama from the wings and gives us a woman's view of it in her autobiography, *After All Is Said and Done*, but she was out front in her efforts to raise civic and cultural life to a higher level. Her legacy to provide "lectures of the very highest type of scholarship which will aid in the permanent preservation of the values of southern culture, history and literature" has enabled Mercer University to bring outstanding scholars to its campus and to establish this series of studies in southern literature, history, and politics. The university will be eternally grateful to this friend who, were she alive today, would welcome the changes for the better but would chide us if we failed to cherish the good in the culture she knew. The Lamar Lectures Committee holds sacred this trust and feels that the studies resulting from the lecture series do make a worthwhile contribution to southern scholarship. Tindall's book holds true to the course of high scholarship which has been maintained now for fourteen years.

SPENCER B. KING, JR., CHAIRMAN,
The Lamar Lectures Committee

Mercer University
Macon, Georgia

Preface

"GARFIELD, ARTHUR, HARRISON, AND HAYES—TIME OF MY father's time, blood of his blood, life of his life. . . . And for me they were the lost Americans: their gravely vacant and bewhiskered faces mixed, melted, swam together in the sea-depths of a past intangible, immeasurable, and unknowable as the buried city of Persepolis." So it seemed to Thomas Wolfe in "The Four Lost Men," a story first published in 1934. And so to a newer generation in the South must seem those remote years of the post-Reconstruction era.

Yet not only have bewhiskered faces come back in style (for students if not for presidents) but the social and political institutions of the South have come back into a state of flux, something like that which existed in the lost years before the triumph of Jim Crow and the Solid South at the turn of the century. The tides move now in a different direction, but the politics of the region are open once again to the strategies of coalition which Garfield, Arthur, Harrison, and Hayes tried to exploit—each in his own way.

The literature about politics in the South since World War II has been until now the province of journalists and political scientists, some of whom have shown great prescience in detecting and projecting trends, but few of whom have explored the longer perspective of historical continuities and parallels.

In the essays which follow I have sought to view recent events in such a perspective. Nevertheless, essays so topical as these must necessarily risk the fallacy of presentism in history. While they were in preparation the phrase "Southern Strategy" was much in the news and the phenomenon of the Nixonian strategy, though not treated in detail here, was much in mind. By some random chance it turned out that the most convenient time to fit the lectures into the schedule of events at Mercer University was November 2–3, 1970, so that the last lecture was given just as the first returns were coming in from the elections of 1970. Fortunately those returns and subsequent events have served more to confirm than to undermine the conclusions already reached. In the process of revision, therefore, the lectures have been altered slightly in style but little in substance.

Lectures so brief can lay no claim to comprehensive treatment of the subject. It can be hoped, however, that they will contribute something to perspectives on recent events and help to open up for more definitive study the significant changes that have occurred in southern politics since World War II.

I am grateful to the Lamar Lectures Committee for the honor of being invited to deliver these lectures, and to the students, faculty, and guests of Mercer University for their warm and attentive reception. I am especially indebted to Professors Spencer B. King, Henry Young Warnock, and Harold L. McManus for hospitalities extended during my stay in Macon. I wish also to express particular appreciation to Professors Andrew and Anne Scott for giving me the germ of the idea for the lectures, to Miss Louise Hall and Mrs. Pattie B. McIntyre of the Louis Round Wilson Library of the University of North Carolina for tracking down elusive references, to Mr. Ralph E. Luker for sharing his copies of the *Ripon Forum*, to Mrs. Betty P. Sawyer of the Institute for Research in Social Science at the University of North Carolina for a careful and expeditious job of typing and to Mrs. John G. Mencke for assistance on the index. Finally, to my wife, Blossom McGarrity Tindall, my most vigilant but loyal critic, must go the credit for saving me from innumerable grotesqueries of style and thought. Those which remain must be attributed to my own obstinacy.

GEORGE B. TINDALL

Chapel Hill, North Carolina
June 1971

ONE

Variations on a Theme by Hayes

THE MORE IT CHANGES THE MORE IT IS THE SAME THING. THAT familiar French proverb is said to have originated with a little-known novelist and political satirist named Alphonse Karr. During the French Revolution of 1848, which eventually swept Napoleon III to power, Karr became oppressed with a sense of watching history repeat itself: "After so many commotions and changes, it is time to recognize one thing, that it is as in a cabaret: green label, red label, etc.— One changes sometimes the price, sometimes the cork, but it is always the same sour wine that one has us drink.—The more it changes—the more it is the same thing."[1]

In the decade of the 1960s southerners, like the Frenchman, could have moments when it seemed as if they had come full cycle to the replay of an historical drama first enacted a century ago. The Civil War centennial remained a period piece played out in costume, without live ammunition. The Reconstruction centennial, however, was staged in modern dress, if a little ahead of schedule. The pageantry was absent: the nation failed to reenact the impeachment of President Johnson and forgot to observe 1970 as the centennial of the Fifteenth Amendment, which guaranteed Negro suffrage. But the parallels lay in something more significant than pageantry, for the controversies of Reconstruction, to a greater degree than those of the Civil War, have remained live issues in the twentieth century.

Some years ago Crane Brinton, in *The Anatomy of Revolution,* sought to chart certain stages and forces common to all revolutions, up to the reaction with which they end.[2] If we could assume a parallel in the anatomy of Reconstruction we might reason that in the late 1960s the civil rights revolution reached the stage of Thermidorean reaction or, by analogy, the Hayes administration with which Reconstruction ended. The parallel is tempting: Rutherford B. Hayes had a Southern Policy; Richard M. Nixon has (or had) a Southern Strategy. The southern strategy, like the southern policy, dictated a posture of benign neglect toward the aspirations of black Americans. It foretokened, therefore, a cycle of reaction and repression. It foretokened, moreover, a new Solid South, this time Republican instead of Democratic, or so one might have conjectured before the midterm elections of 1970.

Such parallels are tempting, and they can serve a useful purpose unless they run out of control. Historical analogy can suggest possibilities and illuminate dangers; it cannot supply a science of prophecy. Our times are so different from the times of Rutherford Hayes that it would be hard to believe that history can follow the same sequence, either in civil rights or in patterns of voting. Perhaps we should not strain the analogy much beyond the point that Nixon like Hayes has sought to cultivate conservative sentiment by relaxing or appearing to relax the commitment to legal rights newly achieved in principle by the black minority. And, in the light of the 1970 elections, with little more success than Hayes.

Cautionary words about historical analogy, however, may be misplaced in the age of pop-art culture. Danger lurks not only in the misuse of historical example, but also in the demand for the relevant, which is often to say the shallow and the ephemeral. This is the great hazard in the social sciences—the "ologies"—sociology, psychology, anthropol-

ogy, and now the newest entry in the field, "psephology."
In the past year this neologism has crept almost undetected
into the American language: "psephology," from a Greek
word meaning "ballots," hence the study of ballots or of
voting behavior. The chief function of this new coinage,
apparently, is to provide a scientific cachet for one of the
major branches of fortunetelling—reading the entrails of
voters and foretelling the outcome of elections, an industry which promises to outstrip Kremlinology in its gross
product.

Recently five major creations have rolled off the psepho-
logical assembly lines, along with countless compact models:
the sensation of 1969 was *The Emerging Republican Majority* by Kevin P. Phillips; last year's wonders were *The
Hidden Crisis in American Politics* by Samuel Lubell and
The Real Majority by Richard C. Scammon and Ben J.
Wattenberg; this year's new models are *The Southern
Strategy* by Reg Murphy and Hal Gulliver and *Changing
Sources of Power: American Politics in the 1970s* by Frederick G. Dutton.[3] *The Emerging Republican Majority,*
widely celebrated as the manifesto of the southern strategy,
proved to be a nine-days' wonder that perfectly illustrated
the hazards of prophecy. Its author, Kevin P. Phillips—a
young lawyer, a former Nixon campaign worker, a former
special assistant to the attorney general, more recently a
columnist—predicted that the true majority in the United
States for the remainder of the twentieth century would be
conservative and Republican, with its bastions in the South
and in the "heartland" of the plains and Rocky Mountains.
A new era had begun, Phillips told the reader: "The long-
range meaning of the political upheaval of 1968 rests on
the Republican opportunity to fashion a majority among
the 57 percent of the American electorate which voted to
eject the Democratic Party from national power"—that is,
the 57 percent who voted for Richard Nixon or George

Wallace.[4] A fitting epigraph for the book, one reviewer thought, would be George Wallace's rallying cry: "They's more of us than they is of them."[5]

Phillips's argument depended first upon a projection of voting trends among ethnic groups, mostly toward the Republican party; second, upon a view that major realignments in American politics have occurred at regular intervals; and third, upon a more dubious argument that the tides of change in American politics have arisen from a South and West in rebellion against successive northeastern establishments (the latest of which is the New Deal-liberal establishment). The first two of these interpretations followed themes currently fashionable among political scientists and historians. One was an emphasis upon ethnic factors in voting—Phillips argued that white ethnic groups had been "trending" away from the Democrats in revulsion against black militants and the "liberal establishment," particularly the establishment's rebellious children. The other theme was the study of "party systems" in American history.

On this Phillips followed what have become fairly standard groupings. For some reason he omitted the Federalist-Jeffersonian Republican system which originated in the 1790s (say, 1796, with the first partisan presidential election); but after that he noted the Democratic-Whig system which arose soon after Andrew Jackson's victory in 1828; the Democratic-Republican system which emerged with Lincoln in 1860; and then without change of party names, the cycle of Republican supremacy after 1896 (the election of McKinley) and Democratic supremacy after 1932 (the election of Franklin D. Roosevelt). This reckoning carried a symmetry that was strangely perfect: five cycles of politics, each lasting thirty-two or thirty-six years, during each of which members of the "out" party occupied the White

House only eight years—in the tenures of the two Adamses, Harrison, Tyler, Cleveland, Wilson, and Eisenhower. Perhaps this denoted some organic cycle of rise and fall—or perhaps another "ology," "numerology"—but Phillips reasoned that every thirty-two or thirty-six years a major realignment occurs in the American political universe. Take 1932, add 36, and one reaches 1968. Richard Nixon, ipso facto, heralded a new cycle of Republican supremacy!

For all the minutiae of ethnic and political history, for all the historical maps and tables and statistics with which Phillips garnished his text, his projections emerged from a shallow perspective in which the future became an extension of the year 1968. If that prospect seems less than appealing we should remember that four years earlier the soothsayers were drawing their projections from the defeat of Barry Goldwater and foretelling the everlasting Democratic majority. Now others will no doubt project the future from 1970. The prudent political prophet, perhaps, must take a cue from J. P. Morgan who, when asked once what the market would do, responded: "It will fluctuate." And indeed all of the more recent books anticipate more fluctuation at the polls than Phillips did. None accepts his proposition that in the long run the Wallace voter belongs to the Republicans, and all question in different ways his judgment about the impact of the "social issue."

The historian, of course, can view all this with a certain wry detachment, for the historian seldom runs the risk of prophecy. He knows, perhaps too well, the snares set for the unwary, the hopes unfulfilled, the trends overlooked, the ironic turns of fortune when events get in the saddle. He may suspect, too, that the turn in Republican fortunes below the Potomac during the last two decades owes less to new strategies than to new conditions, for the southern strategy was not born yesterday. It was invented—or at least first pursued—in the 1870s by Rutherford B. Hayes, who called it his southern policy. Subsequent changes have been only variations on a theme by Hayes.

To understand the southern policy of Hayes, one must turn briefly to still earlier times. The most casual student of political history should know that the antebellum South briefly developed a vigorous two-party competition. Its duration, however, spanned little more than the decade of the 1840s and the party system never became institutionalized. After the Federalists only the short-lived Whig party made a serious challenge to the dominant party, and that for less than two decades.

The Whig party, born of opposition to Andrew Jackson in the 1830s, embraced diverse elements which favored both nationalism and state rights, those who disliked Jackson's rebuffs to the national bank and national roads and those who disliked his rebuff to nullification. In both the North and the South the Whigs had a reputation for respectability, for association with the "broadcloth" element. In the South they included black-belt planters (the "cotton snobs"), urban merchants and bankers, but also (especially in North Carolina) mountaineers who needed roads and supported the party of internal improvements. The southern Whigs soon became, like their northern partners, mainly the partisans of Henry Clay, the Kentucky nationalist who championed an "American System" of tariffs, national bank, and internal improvements—the Great Compromiser who championed sectional peace.

Thus southern Whiggery, while not synonymous with unionism, became permeated with unionism. When sectional controversy over slavery disrupted the Whig party in the 1850s, as it would disrupt the Democratic party in 1860, southern Whigs persisted in efforts to save the union, supported John Bell of Tennessee on the Constitutional

Union ticket in 1860, stood among the foes of secession, and after secession joined the champions of compromise.

The studies of "persistent Whiggery" by Thomas B. Alexander give testimony to the survival of Whiggish sentiments in the Confederacy and on into the postwar South.[6] Whig unionism gained influence as disillusionment with secession mounted, and old Whigs after the war dominated most of the state governments under presidential Reconstruction. At that point, Alexander argues, the southern Whigs missed the chance to shape a national coalition of moderate unionists. Instead of coalition they achieved division when the new state governments under Andrew Johnson passed the restrictive black codes and elected Confederate brigadiers to Congress. Many of the brigadiers were old unionists who had opposed secession, but that point was lost in the polarization between Johnson and the Radical Republicans.

Even so, once the Radical triumph was assured, more than a few Whigs found enough Whiggery in the Republican program to justify support and reasoned that by joining the party they could moderate its more extreme elements. An outstanding example was James L. Alcorn, a conservative planter who became the first Republican governor of Mississippi before he lost out to a Negro-carpetbagger faction. Most of the old Whigs, however, found themselves reluctantly drawn to the Democratic party, which commonly reorganized under the name Conservative to accommodate the new recruits. "The circumstances now surrounding the *South*," wrote the editor of Mississippi's *Hinds County Gazette* in 1868, ". . . are of such vast importance, and the lines so fairly drawn between the Radicals and Democrats, that the Whigs of the South cannot do otherwise than vote with the Democrats, though they do so under protest."[7] Northern Republicans, as well as southern Democrats, assumed a Whiggish cast with the waning of Reconstruction.

In 1876–1877 the circumstances of the disputed presidential election made possible an effort to bring this harmony of outlook into play, to split off southern Democrats from northern, and arrange the compromise which permitted Hayes to become president, instead of Samuel J. Tilden.

The elements of compromise need only brief review here.[8] The dispute turned on contested electoral votes from three southern states—Florida, Louisiana, and South Carolina. The framers of the Constitution did not anticipate the question, and Congress was divided between a Republican senate and Democratic house. A special Electoral Commission, unique in American history, recommended a decision for Hayes, but house Democrats threatened a filibuster, whereupon friends of Hayes and a group of southerners met in the Wormley House, a Washington hotel, to strike a bargain: the southerners would let Hayes take office and would accept in good faith the Reconstruction amendments; Hayes in turn would remove federal troops protecting Republican state governments in South Carolina and Louisiana. Behind this agreement, however, lay more complicated economic and political understandings about federal aid for the Texas and Pacific Railroad, money for internal improvements in the South, a cabinet appointment for a southerner, and a more tenuous agreement for Republican James A. Garfield to become speaker of the house despite a thin Democratic majority.

In retrospect, the sequel to the compromise seems inevitable. Yet the new president had shown enough pragmatism to suggest that in different circumstances he might have pursued different options. A moderate antislavery Whig who joined the Republicans and fought for the Union, Hayes had voted with the Radicals in Congress, but later expressed disillusionment with Reconstruction policies. As governor of Ohio he became known as a reformer but remained loyal to Ulysses Grant. Before his nomination for president he spoke of the need for sectional reconciliation, but during the campaign encouraged party leaders to wave the "bloody shirt." "Our strong ground is the dread of a solid South, rebel rule, etc., etc.," he wrote to James G. Blaine. "I hope you will make these topics prominent in your speeches. It leads people away from 'hard times' which is our deadliest foe."[9] The campaign betrayed little hint of the southern policy Hayes would pursue as president.

When the first returns signaled a defeat, Hayes confessed: "I do not care for myself . . . but I do care for the poor colored men of the South. . . . The Southern people will practically treat the constitutional amendments as nullities, and then the colored man's fate will be worse than when he was in slavery."[10] By this Hayes meant to predict the result of a Democratic victory; ironically he had predicted the result of his own. The circumstances of the electoral dispute soon put Hayes in a posture of conciliation toward southern Democrats and thereby pushed him toward a policy that perhaps better fitted his temperament than his convictions.[11]

Once inaugurated, he set about appeasing southern whites—largely, it turned out, by deserting southern blacks. Federal troops withdrew from the state houses in South Carolina and Louisiana. David M. Key, a Tennessean of conservative bent, became postmaster general and directed a patronage policy that decimated Republican organizations in the South. A policy which confirmed, if it did not induce, the collapse of the Republican party became quickly rationalized as an effort to rebuild the party on a new basis. By stressing a Whiggish policy of internal improvements and sectional peace, Hayes reasoned, and by naming respectable whites to federal offices, he could lure enough intelligent and propertied whites (especially old Whigs and Unionists) to transform the Republican Party, but without losing the support of the freedmen. More hope than policy, perhaps, the plan resembled the contemporary program of

Benjamin Disraeli, who sponsored an alliance of the British gentry and masses in a national party which played both ends against the middle. When Hayes advised blacks in Atlanta that their "rights and interests would be safer if . . . intelligent white men were let alone by the general government," he expressed not so much a platitude as a real trust that white men of intelligence and property would behave with equity toward the less fortunate.[12] More than that he reasoned that division in the white vote and competition for the black vote would best protect human rights in the long run. "The whites must be divided there," Hayes wrote in his diary, "before a better state of things will prevail."[13]

It was not an ignoble design, but neither was it an idea whose time had come. It was an idea whose time had passed with the advent of Radical Reconstruction. Whatever opportunity may have existed in 1865 had dissolved in the next twelve years. The southern policy of Hayes proposed a shift in attitudes, allegiances, and party labels too sudden to be achieved. The Republican organizations in the South—stricken by defeat, starved for patronage, and hostile to his purpose—gave Hayes little or no machinery with which to pursue his goal. Thus his southern policy proved to be all strategy and no tactics.

Its effect was to dishearten Republicans and embolden Democrats who busily reinforced their control. Federal appointments seduced few Democrats. In fact appointees often affirmed their Democratic allegiance the more fiercely, in self-defense. As if to compound the irony, black-belt Democrats soon effected the very alliance of top and bottom that Hayes had sought. In some areas their economic and social power enabled white Democrats to preside over a controlled black electorate. The party of white supremacy paradoxically would soon use black votes to overcome white majorities that favored Independents and Populists.

Hayes's design to dish the Democrats barely survived

the summer of 1877. In September he made a swing through the middle South, accompanied much of the way by South Carolina's Governor Wade Hampton, meeting large and sympathetic audiences. But the euphoria soon faded. The honeymoon was over in October, when Congress met in special session and southern Democrats failed to permit Garfield's election as speaker. After that Hayes expressed second thoughts about a Texas and Pacific Railroad subsidy. From that point the spirit of conciliation dissipated.

In 1878 the southern hill country caught an infection of farm radicalism from the West. The fever of greenback doctrine passed, only to rise again in later years, but it affected southern Democrats enough to immunize them against the Whiggish appeals of Hayes, defender of sound currency and the public credit. During the spring of 1878 house Democrats began to investigate the previous elections. They meant to embarrass Hayes, but the attempt boomeranged when the Republicans produced certain cipher dispatches which incriminated Democrats in efforts to bring pressure against election officials.

Meanwhile Hayes met growing hostility from stalwart Republicans like Senators Roscoe Conkling and William E. Chandler. The president, said the abolitionist William Lloyd Garrison, "sits in his magisterial chair, serene, smiling, complacent, and confident that the best way to protect sheep from being devoured is to give them over to the custody of the wolves. . . ."[14] As if to confirm the observation, southern Democrats rejected conciliation and revived their bulldozing tactics in the midterm elections, and a nearly solid South emerged. In the former Confederacy state governments remained Democratic and the number of Republican congressmen fell from ten to three. Republicans bore losses in both white and black counties. In the deep South they reached virtual collapse.

Hayes confided to his diary regret "that the better ele-

ments of the South were not . . . organized." A week after
the elections he confessed to a reporter: *"I am reluctantly
forced to admit that the experiment was a failure.* The first
election of importance held since it was attempted has
proved that fair elections with free suffrage for every voter
in the South are an impossibility under the existing condition of things."[15] Whatever his intention, the southern
strategy of Hayes had served little purpose except to cover
his retreat. It ratified the collapse of southern Republicanism and did little to mollify the Democrats who turned
their backs on conciliation. After the midterm elections
they forced Hayes onto the defensive just to salvage the re-
maining shreds of federal protection for the right to vote.
Their special target was the Federal Elections Act of 1871,
which authorized federal deputy marshals and supervisors
to observe elections and report alleged frauds to the courts.
In 1877 a Republican senate had blocked the first attempt
to repeal this safeguard, but from 1879 to 1881 the Democratic congress passed eight repeal bills, each of which Hayes
vetoed. Reluctant to forego at least the principle of protection, Hayes remained adamant on this point, but federal
supervision of elections survived only as a feeble gesture
until finally repealed under Cleveland in 1894.

Both North and South drifted back into the mood of sectionalism, and Stalwarts rallied to their old banner. "The
bloody shirt," William Lloyd Garrison insisted. *"In hoc
signo vinces."*[16] And in that sign James A. Garfield con-
quered. *The Republican Campaign Text Book for 1880*
gave more than half its space to "bloody shirt" themes, and
party propaganda played on the fear of unreconstructed
rebels. But the tone was defensive. There was no commitment to a renewed Reconstruction. The answer to a Solid
South would be simply a Solid North. In 1880 the vote produced a Solid South in the electoral college for the first
time after the Civil War—and very nearly a Solid North

beyond the border states, except for California, Nevada, and New Jersey.

The first major variation on the strategy of Hayes occurred under his immediate successors. Where circumstances impelled Hayes to bid for conservative support, circumstances impelled Garfield and Chester A. Arthur to fraternize with economic radicals. The political independents who sprang up in the South after Reconstruction had little in common with orthodox Republicans except opposition to the Democrats. They endorsed a variety of heterodox proposals: debt repudiation, inflation, usury laws, antimonopoly laws. Locally they fought Bourbon Democrats over fencing laws, the dominance of courthouse rings, and a variety of personal complaints. In Virginia, where the Readjuster movement championed reduction of the state debt, independents captured the legislature in 1879 and elected a governor in 1881. When the Readjusters sent their leader, William E. Mahone, to the United States Senate, he found himself suddenly the key figure in a chamber evenly divided between the parties. To win his vote, senate Republicans came to terms, and Garfield came across with a share of the federal patronage.

When Arthur became president in the fall of 1881 he broadened this qualified alliance into a policy of wholesale collaboration. "I have made up my mind that a permanently defeated Republican party is of little value . . . ," Arthur said, "and that if any respectable body of men wages war on the Bourbon Democracy, with reasonable prospects of success, it should be sustained."[17] In nearly every southern state Arthur fed patronage to independents and urged Republicans to collaborate in their campaigns. In 1882 the alliance showed promise. Eight Republicans went to Congress and eight independents, double the number two years before, but six of the independents were from Virginia, where the Readjusters lost control the following year. In

1884 all the independent congressmen lost, along with Republican presidential candidate James G. Blaine, who polled a smaller proportion of the southern vote than either Hayes or Garfield.

Out of power under Grover Cleveland, Republicans vacillated between waving the bloody shirt and cultivating support for the protective tariff among New South businessmen. In 1888 Benjamin Harrison eschewed the bloody shirt and emphasized protectionism, but in winning polled a still smaller part of the southern vote than Blaine. In 1890, having concluded that Republicans lost in the South mainly because they could not register their full strength at the polls, Harrison threw his support behind one final drive to protect the voting rights of southern Negroes. A federal elections bill, sponsored by Congressman Henry Cabot Lodge of Massachusetts, proposed to give federal supervisors power to control registration and pass on the qualifications of challenged voters. The "Force Bill," as Democrats tagged it, passed the house on a party-line vote, but was sidetracked in the senate to make way for silver and tariff bills and was finally defeated. The will to regulate southern elections was lacking.

In 1892, when discontents of farmers South and West gave rise to the People's party, Harrison had one more chance to cultivate an independent rebellion. In his campaign for reelection the Republican national committee sought to coordinate Republican and Populist groups, but the fusion failed to show much strength in a key test—the Georgia state elections in October—in which Populists lost out to wholesale manipulation by Democrats. Harrison was reported to have greeted the news in a furious rage. "I have washed my hands of the south," he told a visitor, if we may believe the *Atlanta Constitution*. "It is a land of rebels and traitors who care nothing for the sanctity of the ballot, and I will never be in favor of making an active campaign down there until we can place bayonets at the polls. I am now more than ever in favor of ramming a force bill down their throats."[18] Harrison himself lost the election in November.

In four years Benjamin Harrison had recapitulated the whole schizophrenic history of southern strategies. He tried everything again, and again nothing worked. First, a variation on Hayes's appeal to the conservatives, with focus on the protective tariff. Second, a return to Radicalism with the Lodge bill, which failed to pass. And, finally, a return to the Garfield-Arthur strategy of collaboration with independents, in this case with the Populists. Republican vacillation and failure were the products of many circumstances: disillusionment with Reconstruction, factional divisions, a growing doctrine of racial distinctions, the influence of northern businessmen with southern connections, the various social and cultural movements toward sectional reconciliation, which generally meant reconciliation of whites to the disadvantage of blacks.

But the persistent neglect of black Republicans won few points with southern whites. Republicans could not reshape the image they had acquired in the sectional conflict. They were the northern party which had opposed the right of the South to carry slaves into the territories. They had waged war on the South, freed the slaves, and imposed Radical Reconstruction. During the debate over the Lodge bill in 1890 a group of southern congressmen hastily assembled a little volume entitled *Why the Solid South?*[19] The answer they gave in 452 pages can be summarized in one word— Reconstruction. State by state they reviewed that period in terms that would shape the image of Reconstruction history for more than fifty years. Indeed one measure of the Republican burden was the degree to which the terminology of Democratic propaganda dominated political discourse and entered historiography: carpetbagger, scalawag, home rule (as a euphemism for white supremacy), the bloody shirt, outrage mills (a jocose term for reports of political violence and murder), Force Bill, bayonets, Negro domination.

Despite Harrison's failure southern Republicans kept toying with Populist alliances. In 1892 Republicans in Alabama and Louisiana arranged fusions with Populists and in other states gave their informal support or endorsement. Here and there well-known Republican names appeared on Populist tickets and local fusions occurred. In Alabama, which proved to be the banner Populist state of the South in 1892 (36.6 percent of its presidential vote for the Populists), the "Jeffersonian Democrat" Reuben F. Kolb had Populist and Republican support for governor. In the end he lost out on the vote from black-belt counties, which the Democrats controlled. The same thing would happen again in 1894. Throughout the South in the 1892 and subsequent elections Populists fell victim to invective, intimidation, ballot-box stuffing, vote-buying, physical violence. "We had to do it!" one Georgia Democrat said years later. "Those d——— Populists would have ruined the country!"[20]

Populism reached and passed its climax in 1896, when the Democrats under William Jennings Bryan ran off with the issue of free silver. The Populist decision to support Bryan placed southern Populists in the impossible situation of favoring a Democratic candidate for president while collaborating with Republicans at the state level. In Georgia, Alabama, and Texas, Populist state tickets with Republican help polled over 40 percent of the votes even as reported by Democratic boards. In Louisiana a Republican gubernatorial candidate on a fusionist ticket probably was counted out. But in North Carolina, where fusion had carried the legislature in 1894, a new election law made it possible for fusionists to register their full strength. A straightout Republican governor was elected, a fusionist state ticket, a fusionist legislature, and four Populist and three Republican congressmen (the House later seated a fifth Populist in a contested election). But North Carolina Democrats mobilized on the issue of white supremacy in 1898, swept the fusionists out of the legislature and went on to elect a governor in 1900.

Populism therefore never came to power in a single southern state, and the threat posed by fusionists in the 1890s impelled the Democrats to tighten their control, to disfranchise Negro Republicans by literacy tests and other requirements and by the establishment of white primaries. The Solid South, having subdued Republicans, Independents, and Populists, would not face another sustained threat until the mid-twentieth century.

William McKinley's campaign for president illustrated perfectly the standard uses of what had become the rotten boroughs of Republicanism in the South. His campaign may almost be said to have originated in the South, at Thomasville, Georgia, whence McKinley repaired to the vacation home of his strategist Mark Hanna in 1895 to consult quietly with southern Republicans and line up convention delegates before other candidates realized what was afoot. The strategy scored a brilliant success, but McKinley's election in 1896, which began a cycle of Republican supremacy in the nation, left the Solid South without any sustained challenge until the mid-twentieth century. Indebted to southern delegates for convention votes, McKinley outdid his predecessors in the appointment of token Negroes to office, but made little effort to develop a southern strategy for elections. During southern tours in 1898 and 1901 his appeals to white southerners were either sentimental pleas for reunion or prophecies of a rich future. "Sectional lines no longer mar the map of the United States," he told the Georgia legislature a few months after the Spanish-American War. "The old flag again waves over us in peace, with new glories which your sons and ours have added this year to its sacred folds." In the same speech he asserted the care of Confederate graves to be a national duty.[21]

McKinley's successor, Theodore Roosevelt, had the distinction of a southern ancestry—his mother was one of the Georgia Bullochs. But the advantage greatly diminished after Booker T. Washington came to dinner at the White House in 1901. Shortly after that incident Roosevelt wrote to Henry Cabot Lodge: "In the Southern Atlantic and Gulf States there has really been no Republican Party . . . simply a set of black and white scalawags . . . who are concerned purely in getting the Federal offices and sending to the national conventions delegates whose venality makes them a menace to the whole party."[22] But Roosevelt like McKinley found that expediency required him to cultivate the existing organizations to win renomination. His most conspicuous acts in that connection, aside from public acknowledgment of Washington as patronage advisor, were to appoint a Negro, William D. Crum, as collector of customs in Charleston and to close the post office in Indianola, Mississippi, after mob threats had forced the black postmistress to resign.

In 1905, after he had won election to a full term, Roosevelt tried to repair the damage among southern whites by a tour of the South, during which he eulogized General Lee and visited the ancestral Bulloch home at Roswell, but the wide popularity that he achieved won no significant political gains. "The way of Roosevelt with the South was as tortuous as the proverbial way of a man with a maid," C. Vann Woodward has written. "Simultaneously, or by turns, he wooed the mutually hostile Black-and-Tans, Lily-whites, and White-Supremacy Democrats." But whites could not forget Washington's dinner at the White House, and Negroes lost faith when Roosevelt summarily discharged three companies of black troops in 1906 after a riot in Brownsville, Texas. For all his bluster Roosevelt, like his predecessors, vacillated and drifted still further toward a lily-white policy. Later, when he organized the Progressive party in 1912, the Bull Moose convention refused to seat any Negro delegates from the South.[23]

Under William Howard Taft a brief but illusory gain in southern Republicanism occurred. The growth of the industrial New South continued to enlarge the business groups sympathetic to Republican policies on currency and the tariff, and hostile to the populistic Democracy of William Jennings Bryan. Southern publicists like William Garrott Brown and Walter Hines Page began to call for a dissolution of the Solid South. In October 1908 Taft became the first presidential candidate of his party to carry his campaign into the South—on a tour through Kentucky, Tennessee, North Carolina, and Virginia. The Republican vote increased significantly in those and other southern states, and even brought Taft close to victory in Tennessee and North Carolina. North Carolina sent three Republicans to Congress. Taft ventured a prediction after the election that three or four southern states would go Republican in the next election and in a speech assured the North Carolina Society of New York that Republicans would not interfere with Negro disfranchisement.

In 1909 an extensive tour carried Taft into every southern state except Florida, but mainly for ceremonial occasions at which he, like McKinley, gave audiences what they wanted to hear—praise of southern traditions and southern heroes. Taft nominated southern Democrats to federal offices, appointed fewer Negroes than any of his predecessors, called upon southern businessmen to support Republican economic policies, and openly endorsed white supremacy; but his position on the tariff proved highly unpopular in the region, and Democrats swept the midterm elections. Taft's personal popularity in the South, like Roosevelt's, produced no political gains. In 1912 the nation turned to

Woodrow Wilson, the first Democratic president elected since 1892, with comfortable majorities throughout the South.[24]

In 1920 the landslide victory of Warren G. Harding brought another rise in the southern Republican vote, enough to carry the state of Tennessee, probably because the party won credit for the state's ratification of woman suffrage. "Mr. Harding thinks the time is ripe for dissolving the Solid South," the still-hopeful William Howard Taft reported after the election. But Harding remained impaled on the horns of the old Republican dilemma: how to combine a growing white vote with a traditional black vote. With some apparent hope that he could find the formula to pick up a few more Negro votes without antagonizing whites, Harding seized upon the semicentennial celebration of Birmingham, Alabama, in 1921 as the occasion for a speech on the race question. The strategy was to "stand uncompromisingly against every suggestion of social equality" but to argue that the black man should vote "when he is fit to vote" and have equal opportunities "in precisely the same way and to the same extent . . . as between members of the same race." Even so mild, almost platitudinous, a speech met widespread hostility among both whites and blacks, and it effected little or no change in the political situation.[25] After Harding's death Calvin Coolidge said even less on the subject. Both men endorsed federal anti-lynching bills, but neither restored Negro patronage to pre-Wilson levels or moved against the segregation established in government offices under Wilson. And neither acted with any vigor to devise a southern strategy.[26]

The story of Republican efforts to build a party in the South, then, was a story of futility, a futility born chiefly of the failure of Reconstruction. Republicans over the years progressively abandoned the Radical tradition which, however, still hung like an albatross around their necks. Republican presidents appointed southern Democrats to federal office, neglected southern Negroes, and called on the New South to support their economic policies. But the more it changed the more it was the same thing. The more Republicans abandoned the black man the more they failed with the white. Yet all Republican presidents remained dependent for convention votes upon regular organizations that included Negroes, and ambivalence about Negro Republicans continued.

Not until the mid-twentieth century would the southern policy of Rutherford B. Hayes begin to score success. That would come with Dwight D. Eisenhower, but less because of any new southern strategy than because of new conditions which afflicted the Democrats with severe internal tensions. In the 1930s the New Deal undermined the Republican loyalties of black voters and created a new tradition of black Democrats. Among southern whites this and other departures by the New Deal eroded loyalties born of Civil War and Reconstruction and brought on a disruption of southern Democracy. This in turn would reinvigorate the southern strategy that had failed so repeatedly in the years before.

TWO

The Disruption of Southern Democracy

"THE 'SOLID SOUTH'—LONG THE FETICH OF ONE SECTION OF the country and the bugaboo of the other—has at last been shattered to such a degree that all the king's horses and men of the nursery rhyme could not put it together again, and with its destruction there vanishes from the field of American politics the long and bitter struggle over the slavery question." That statement by historian Burr J. Ramage, which appeared in the *Sewanee Review* for August 1896, belongs to a durable tradition of clouded prophecy.[1]

Almost from the birth of the Solid South reports of its death flew on every shifting breeze of politics. "I am looking every year for a break-up of the Solid South," Henry Watterson of the *Louisville Courier-Journal* wrote in 1887. The third nomination of Grover Cleveland "snapped the last cord which binds free men to the Democratic party," said Robert Beverly, Jr., of Virginia in 1892. Different southerners reacted the same way to William Jennings Bryan. In 1908 Walter Hines Page welcomed "the impending and inevitable breaking of the Solid South" when he introduced William Howard Taft to the North Carolina Society of New York. In 1909 Enoch M. Banks foresaw "The Passing of the Solid South" in the *South Atlantic Quarterly*. In 1910 James W. Garner predicted a "New Politics for the South" in the *Annals of the American Academy*.[2] The rise of Populism in the 1890s, the bolt of the Hoovercrats in 1928, reaction against the New Deal in the 1930s and 1940s —all gave rise to predictions of imminent breakup.

Such predictions usually went in tandem with a rationale that editor-historian Douglas Southall Freeman expressed in the 1920s: "There is no progress without opposition, and no opposition without dissent. Virginia has long been in danger of political stagnation."[3] The rigid solidarity of the South, according to a common and persistent opinion, downgraded issues and programs, encouraged a politics of personalities, gave rise to demagogues, fostered neglect and nonvoting, and reduced the region's influence in both national parties. Such opinion, however, seldom led to action. Discussions of one-party stagnation, Rupert Vance once said, often ended on some such note as: "We need a two-party system. Why don't *you* become a Republican?"

Neither the prophecies nor the rationale of a two-party system perceptibly hastened the fall of the Solid South. It was a lingering end, but it did finally come, and the historian can now file the death certificate. The time of death, like the time of birth, cannot be established exactly. But if we reckon by presidential vote, the life-span of the Solid South fell just short of the Biblical three score and ten—a period of sixty-eight years from 1880 to 1948. Since the Dixiecrat rebellion of 1948 the former Confederate states have not cast a solid electoral vote in a single election. Before that date, unless one counts the border states or the singular case of Tennessee in 1920, the only deviation was the Hoovercrat rebellion against Al Smith in 1928.

The persistent gains of the Republican party after 1948, however, owe less to any deliberate southern strategy of the party than to the persistent disruption of the Democratic party, which after all has much the longer record of successful "northern men with southern principles," reaching back to the earliest days of the Republic, but has also a record of such turbulence as to lend much truth to Will Rogers' classic disavowal: "I am a member of no organized political party. I am a Democrat." The source of trouble has been the uneasy alliance of incongruous elements ever since Jefferson and Madison in the 1790s formed the partnership between southern agrarians and Tammany Hall. In phrases that would evoke the envy of the polysyllabic Spiro Agnew, John Hay once called the Democratic party "a fortuitous concourse of unrelated prejudices" and H. L. Mencken described it as "two gangs of natural enemies in a precarious state of symbiosis."

At few times in the history of the party had such descriptions been more pertinent than in the 1920s. The election of Warren Harding in 1920 marked the end of that remarkable coalition of agrarians, laborites, and reformers that Woodrow Wilson had assembled during his first term. Dissolution of the Wilsonian synthesis had been signaled by the congressional elections of 1918, in which sectional resentment of the special consideration given to cotton prices caused the Democrats to lose control of Congress at the critical point of peace negotiations. Thereafter the multiple tensions of demobilization and peacemaking poisoned the postwar political climate and contributed to an urge for normalcy.[4]

The reform spirit of progressivism, which had pervaded the politics of the prewar decades, was shattered by the new spirit of the times. In much of the country, especially the South, the impulse for reform turned into a drive for moral righteousness and conformity. Prohibition, the Ku Klux Klan, and the fundamentalist movement inherited the reform spirit but channeled it into new crusades which fed upon the anxieties of the uprooted newcomers in growing southern towns. For the liberated smart set it was a time of revolt against the village mind, against the conventions of Main Street, against the rustic virtues—a time of short skirts, bobbed hair, flaming youth, and bathtub gin. The clash of different "life styles" made it a time, indeed, much like the late 1960s.

Thus a deep alienation, compounded with no little intolerance on both sides, isolated the provincial South from the metropolis. The decade of the 1920s saw a significant revival of sectional consciousness. The concept of the South as a conscious minority—the defensive concept of the embattled South standing off the infidels—had taken form in the nineteenth-century sectional conflict. It has been endemic ever since, and like many other social myths it has been a potent force in human affairs. It is not, of course, the only idea of what the South was and is—or might be— but it is one that, lying dormant, quickly revives in the heat of controversy and it is one that has flourished in recent years.

The discontents of the 1920s found their focus in the Democratic party partly because Republicans faced no divisive struggles for the presidential nomination but more because the Democrats encompassed the more extreme differences between the metropolitan and rural-small-town viewpoints. The split in the Wilsonian coalition found expression in the rival candidacies of Alfred E. Smith and William Gibbs McAdoo in the convention of 1924. It reached a climax in disagreement over a proposal to name the Ku Klux Klan in a plank denouncing bigotry, which led to the symbolic spectacle of the aging William Jennings Bryan goaded and heckled by Tammany gallants in the galleries of Madison Square Garden. McAdoo and Smith canceled each other out, and it took 103 ballots to bestow a badly tarnished nomination on John W. Davis. Four years later the withdrawal of McAdoo left no real alternative to Al Smith, but as a Tammanyite, Catholic son of an Irish immigrant, and a wet, a New Yorker who spoke with a curious twang on the "raddio," Smith personified for southerners all the alien qualities of the metropolis.

The election returns of 1928 recorded a sharp division in the Solid South. That election has undergone endless analyses and judgments, mostly focused on the relative significance of the prohibition and Catholic issues. But the two things became so completely tangled with each other and with nebulous fears of the alien city that one can hardly unravel the snarl. Less noticed but more pregnant with meaning for the future was the geographical pattern of racial and economic issues. Only the deep South—Louisiana, Mississippi, Alabama, Georgia, and South Carolina, together with Arkansas—remained Democratic. The decisive factor, except perhaps in Arkansas, home of Smith's running mate, was a revival of the race issue with dire warnings against splitting the white vote.

In the deep South racial prejudice simply outweighed religious prejudice. In the outer South a more potent force was the nascent middle-class Republicanism in the cities and suburbs. "Republican rolls, once dedicated to niggers, hillbillies and other such pariahs," W. J. Cash wrote, "begin to smack of the Social Register."[5] In the election Herbert Hoover captured centers of the New South spirit like Houston, Dallas, Birmingham, Atlanta, Chattanooga, and Richmond while Smith held the more tradition-bound cities like San Antonio, New Orleans, Mobile, Montgomery, Savannah, Charleston, and Memphis. "The aristocrat still exists," wrote a southern-born professor at Princeton, "he derides the antievolution laws, denounces the interference of the preachers in politics, and glorifies the party of Jefferson and Jackson. But it is the great new middle class, the heirs to the vigorous, prosperous, advancing New South, who now decide the elections."[6]

Before the election Herbert Hoover shunned the black-

and-tan Republicans and cultivated white "Hoovercrats." After the election he sought to foster in the South a lily-white Republicanism "of such character as would commend itself to the citizens of those states." Again the southern strategy of Rutherford Hayes experienced one of its periodic revivals and again the black-and-tan regulars suffered a setback.[7] But again unforeseen events intervened. In 1929 Hoover, the herald of prosperity, fell victim to the stock market crash, and the party of Reconstruction became also the party of Depression. The misfortunes of Herbert Hoover operated to discredit the peculiar forces that had combined to oppose Al Smith in 1928: prohibition, fundamentalism, nativism, religious bigotry—and the nascent middle-class Republicanism. Their embarrassment helped clear the way for the New Deal. Prominent Hoovercrats went down to defeat in the next election, and the South returned to Democratic solidarity. Momentarily sectional defensiveness lay dormant.

Automatic southern hostility toward the man who occupies the White House, whomever he might be, has not been a phenomenon of all times—familiar as it has been in recent decades. It was not so with either of the first two Democratic presidents of the twentieth century, both of whom leaned heavily on Southern support. Woodrow Wilson, himself southern-born, presided over a cabinet half of whom were born south of the Potomac, and he put his progressive program through a Congress dominated by southern committee chairmen. Wilson drew southern leaders into the orbit of national and international affairs to a degree unknown since the Civil War.

Much the same process occurred during the first term of Franklin D. Roosevelt. Roosevelt was not a southerner, but he had a second home in Georgia. Many southerners again held high office and dominated committee chairmanships. Roosevelt, like Wilson, relied upon their parliamentary skills to push his programs through Congress. And on international affairs he retained their support, with few exceptions, to the very end.

For the South the New Deal decade was a period of unusually active ferment, intellectual as well as social and political—a ferment from which it seemed possible, even likely, that an entirely new vision of the regional identity might arise. It was the period of the Vanderbilt agrarians and the Chapel Hill regionalists, a period during which the southern renaissance in literature reached maturity, and these were only the most conspicuous manifestations of a new regional consciousness that inspired a great body of social and economic analysis and an extensive literature of social exploration and descriptive journalism.

Yet, despite all the activity of the literati in rediscovering, analyzing, interpreting the South, a broad chasm separated them from the region's leaders. "If Southern people of the ruling orders read the Southern novelists but little," Cash wrote in *The Mind of the South*, "they read the studies which were concerned with the questions directly involved in the cotton-population-unemployment quandary of the South hardly at all," and they dismissed them as "the work of busy-body theorists bent on raising disturbing issues." There was "no articulation between the new intellectual leaders and the body of the South, and it is in this that the tragedy of the South as it stood in 1940 centrally resided."[8]

So the discussion of southern problems had a way of slipping back into time-worn channels. The South's political leaders, in detachment from its intellectual leaders (but it should be added, abetted by some of its intellectual leaders) exploited a resurgent sectionalism, fought for equalization of freight rates, pursued defense and war industries, argued issues of race that assumed new urgency during World War II, opposed New Deal labor and welfare measures. The new regionalism gradually dissolved into the old sectionalism, from which southern conservatives forged destructive weapons against the New Deal.

Roosevelt increasingly acquired enemies. Nearly every program to which the New Deal addressed itself seemed inadvertently designed to raise sectional opposition. New Deal crop limitations antagonized the cotton trade, NRA codes and labor standards annoyed industrialists, relief policies raised the question of regional wage differentials. Sectional feeling, which had strengthened the coalitions of Bryan and Wilson, plagued Roosevelt as it had plagued his party in the 1920s. Unlike Wilson's New Freedom, Roosevelt's New Deal challenged the social and economic power structures of the South, and thereby provoked an opposition such as Wilson never had—and created a loyalty among the rank and file such as Wilson never had.

The roots of rebellion lay in the county-seat elites, in what political scientist Jasper Shannon labeled the "banker-merchant-farmer-lawyer-doctor-governing class," and what Ralph McGill called "a certain type, small-town rich man."[9] In McGill's description this village nabob

owned, according to his geographic location, the gin, the turpentine works, the cotton warehouses, the tobacco warehouses. He was a director in the bank.

He was the owner of all, or part of, the biggest store. . . .

At least one of the popular automobile agencies was in his name, or owned by a brother, uncle, or son.

He controlled credit. . . .

He was, more often than not, a deacon in his church. If not a deacon, he was a "pillar," in that he gave liberally. . . .

He usually owned and operated a few farms, taken in on foreclosures.

This certain type, small-town rich man hated Roosevelt,

the New Deal, the triple A, and the Federal Land Bank, which took mortgages and farm loans out of his hands.
He damned the WPA because it took away farm labor.
He hated all union labor. . . . He did not want new industries in "his" town. They competed for "his" labor.
He fondly regarded himself as the bulwark of all that was "best" and of the Southern "traditions."

For these people the New Deal jeopardized a power that rested on the control of property, labor, credit, and local government. Relief projects reduced dependency; labor standards raised wages; farm programs upset landlord-tenant relationships; government credit bypassed bankers; new federal programs skirted county commissioners and sometimes even state agencies.

The trends became more ominous in 1935, when the "Second New Deal" swung from recovery to reform with such measures as the WPA, social security, the Wagner Act, the "soak-the-rich" tax, and later, the Farm Tenant and Housing Acts of 1937 and the Fair Labor Standards Act of 1938. "Northernization" of the Democratic Party in the wake of overwhelming victories aggravated the tensions. In 1936 the Democratic convention eliminated the two-thirds rule for nominations, thereby removing the South's veto power, and seated Negro delegates. The grand exit of South Carolina's Senator Cotton Ed Smith from the Philadelphia convention provided a symbolic prelude to the disruption of the Democratic party. In Smith's own words, as remembered by Harry Ashmore from the classic campaign speech on "Phillydelphy":

. . . when I came out on the floor of that great hall, bless God, it looked like a checkerboard—a spot of white here, and a spot of black there. [Actually there were thirty black delegates or alternates.] But I kept going, down that long aisle, and finally I found the great standard of South Carolina—and, praise God, it was in a spot of white!

I had no sooner than taken my seat when a newspaperman came down the aisle and squatted by me and said, "Senator, do you know a nigger is going to come out up yonder in a minute and offer the invocation?" I told him, I said, "Now don't be joking me, I'm upset enough the way it is." But then, bless God, out on that platform walked a slew-footed, blue-gummed, kinky-headed Senegambian!

And he started praying and I started walking. And as I pushed through those great doors, and walked across that vast rotunda, it seemed to me that old John Calhoun leaned down from his mansion in the sky and whispered in my ear, "You did right, Ed. . . ."[10]

Another omen of disruption had appeared earlier the same year in Macon where Governor Eugene Talmadge summoned what he called a "Grass Roots Convention" to rally the anti-New Dealers and incidentally start a boom for Talmadge. Invitations went to "Jeffersonian Democrats" in seventeen southern and border states, but the show played to a half-empty municipal auditorium and drew chiefly the far-right fringes of economic and racial conservatives.

Later, on August 7, a small number of disgruntled southerners helped organize an abortive movement of "Jeffersonian Democrats." In several states the Jeffersonians fielded independent electoral tickets under various names, the "Constitutional Democrats of Texas" making the biggest display, stressing anti-Negro and anti-Communist themes.[11] The movement had little effect on the voters, but it planted in southern politics the idea of independent electors, which has flourished periodically ever since. Beguiled by visions of a deadlocked election, southern ultraconservatives in the face of repeated failures kept alive the dream of another sectional compromise: another Wormley House, another bargain, another Hayes. The technical details would be different from those of 1877, but not the result. Instead of disputed votes the scheme would require an electoral college deadlocked for want of a majority. If no bargain emerged before the electors cast their votes, moreover, it would require a House of Representatives so evenly divided as to give the schemers a balance of power in naming the president. Few politicians could be so bold as to hazard careers on such a speculation.

An effective opposition to Roosevelt did not coalesce until he provoked a constitutional crisis in 1937 with his proposal to reform the courts. The "court-packing" maneuver handed new issues to men who previously had shunned a fight with Roosevelt. Southern congressmen hastened to defend the Court as quickly as they hastened to attack it two decades later. Certain "visionary incendiaries" in the administration, said Virginia's Senator Carter Glass, virtually proposed "another tragic era of reconstruction for the South." Such men "very likely . . . would be glad to see reversed those decisions of the court that saved the civilization of the South."[12]

Roosevelt later claimed that he lost the battle but won the war. The Senate blocked his bill, but the Court changed its interpretation on several important points and a resignation gave Roosevelt the opportunity to name his first appointee, Hugo Black of Alabama. But it was a pyrrhic victory that divided the Democratic party and blighted Roosevelt's prestige. For the first time southern congressmen in large numbers deserted the leader, and the opposition found an issue on which it could openly take the field. Things were never again quite the same.

Even while the court bill pended, southern rebellions erupted on other fronts: against sit-down strikes, against relief spending. Sectional issues continued to rise. Criticism mounted over discriminatory freight rates. Conservatives in the Farm Bureau assailed the tenant program and the demands of organized labor. Anti-lynching bills provoked filibusters. In the New Deal coalition conservative southerners had become uneasy bedfellows with organized labor and Negroes. Consequently some of them drifted toward counter-coalition with conservative Republicans. Before the court battle ended in 1937 the rapprochement was apparent. A conservative bloc, if unorganized and mutable, had appeared. And it held the New Dealers to a virtual stalemate. In 1938 Roosevelt's prestige was further eroded by his failure to "purge" opponents like Senators Walter George of Georgia and Cotton Ed Smith of South Carolina in the party primaries.

In 1940 at least a few southern rebels found in Wendell Willkie a Republican sufficiently heterodox to lessen the curse of his party label. They put out separate tickets in South Carolina and Texas which pledged support to Willkie as the only "real Democrat" in the race. In 1944 independent electors cropped up again, in three states. In South Carolina the "southern Democrats" fielded a ticket pledged to Senator Harry F. Byrd. In Mississippi and Texas rebel elements captured the state conventions and nominated unpledged electors, but Roosevelt swept the field in all three states. The independents made their strongest showing in Texas where the "Texas Regulars" polled 11.8 percent of the vote while the Republicans took 16.8. The figures in South Carolina were 7.5 Independent and 4.5 Republican; in Mississippi 5.5 and 6.4 respectively.[13]

The New Deal, however, sparked another kind of rebellion. Southern New Dealers had a different vision of the political future: an extension into the South of the liberal-labor-Negro coalition to which the New Deal had given rise in the North. This was as much a long shot in its own way as the independent-electors scheme. It required an increase in the voting of low-income groups, and it anticipated that low-income voters would see their self-interest in such a coalition. The "only hope for progressive democracy in the South lies in the lower income groups—particularly the wage earner," labor leader Lucy Randolph Mason wrote to Eleanor Roosevelt. "Yet this is the group so largely disfranchised by the poll-tax requirements of eight Southern states."[14] The prerequisite to a liberal coalition, therefore, was repeal of the poll tax, but efforts to that end met with stubborn resistance and have reached complete success only in recent years. The liberal hope took into account neither the obstacles to the labor movement in the region nor the vulnerability of low-income whites to racial appeals in the coming decades. But like the dream of another sectional bargain the dream of a liberal coalition has had its perennial rebirths.

In the period of World War ii the rising winds of Negro aspirations fanned the flames of racial reaction. A storm of discontent with Negro demands, price controls, labor shortages, rationing, and a hundred other petty vexations reinforced the winds of conservatism. Allen Drury, a young Texan covering the Senate for the United Press, recorded his impressions in 1944: "We seem to be perched on a cliff, in Washington, above a vast and tumbled plain that stretches far away below us: the South, unhappy, restless, confused, embittered, torn by pressures steadily mounting. As far as the eye can see there is discontent and bitterness, faint intimations of a coming storm like a rising wind moving through tall grass."[15]

After the war defensive reactions in the South resembled those after World War i, although the issues were different: stubborn opposition to civil rights, retreat from support of international cooperation, the rise of a radical right. The experience of the 1920s and 1930s suggests that the source of defensive reaction lay mainly in two groups: first, the uprooted and uncertain newcomers to the towns, the people of upward mobility but insecure status whose anxiety arose from the very changes that bettered their condition; and, second, the village nabobs of the small towns—and we might add the new-rich of the larger towns—secure in their local power but filled with anxiety about the winds of change that swept the world. As we move into the final third of the twentieth century, social and economic change may be catching up with these groups, but their presence can still be felt.

The difference, perhaps, lies in the fact that they found common cause. In the 1920s respectable citizens shied away from the Klan and fundamentalism. In the 1930s the people of more insecure status felt the pinch of economic adversity and stood by the New Deal. Since World War II, when economic conditions have been fairly prosperous and the focus has been fairly steadily on issues of race, events have tended to push these groups together, with common anxieties and common targets. Economic conservatism and concerns about status, social issues, and styles of life have reinforced each other.

By 1948 this convergence could be seen in the makeup of the Dixiecrat movement, which under the time-honored code name of states' rights, championed both racial and economic conservatism—with a special concern at the time for Harry Truman's civil rights proposals and the control of tidelands oil. The States' Rights Democrats sprang into existence when the Democratic convention adopted a strong civil rights plank after a plea from Mayor Hubert Humphrey of Minneapolis to "get out of the shadow of states' rights and walk forthrightly into the bright sunlight of human rights. . . ." The Mississippi delegates and half of the Alabama delegates walked out of the convention instead. Later a "conference" of states' righters in Birmingham nominated J. Strom Thurmond of South Carolina for president. Their rebellion gave the fullest opportunity yet for the idea of independent electors, who in 1948 had the advantage of running on the regular Democratic ticket in four states.[16]

By its very character the Dixiecrat movement illustrated the tenacious hold of Democratic loyalty on southern voters. Where the Dixiecrats ran under the regular party emblem they won; elsewhere they lost. But the states in which they captured the machinery were not a matter of random chance. The pattern of 1948 stood the pattern of 1928 on its head. The Dixiecrats triumphed in Alabama, Louisiana, Mississippi, and South Carolina, the very states that twenty years before had provided the core of party loyalty, together with Georgia and Arkansas. Moreover, and not incidentally, these states had been among the first to secede in 1860–1861; they would in turn fit the Goldwater pattern in 1964, with Georgia but without Arkansas, and the Wallace pattern in 1968, with Arkansas and Georgia but without South Carolina. The deep South—that is, a group of states from Louisiana eastward through South Carolina—has remained the seat of southern white intransigence, the area in which politics has turned more on race than in the outer South, and the hard core has been Alabama, Mississippi, and Louisiana.

The Dixiecrats of 1948, then, differed sharply from the Hoovercrats of 1928. And the sequel was different: 1948, unlike 1928, was the start of an ongoing rebellion. Since that time the South has split its electoral vote in five presidential elections, and in two of these it has divided three ways. It has experienced a sizeable growth of presidential Republicanism; and in the 1960s a breakthrough in congressional, state, and local Republicanism.

For a while it seemed likely that the Dixiecrats would go the way of the Hoovercrats. Indeed, as a formally organized group they did. In 1949 a nucleus of the faithful observed the movement's first anniversary in a meeting at

Jackson, Mississippi, where they formed a National States' Rights Committee mainly for propaganda purposes. Only a remnant appeared for the next annual conference in 1950. Their leader, Strom Thurmond, by then was already engaged in a losing battle to unseat Senator Olin D. Johnston. From the start southern members of Congress had kept their distance in order to preserve their party standing and seniority. Outside the deep South core the 1948 primaries had produced leaders well to the left of the Dixiecrats: Governor Sid McMath in Arkansas, Governor Gordon Browning and Senator Estes Kefauver in Tennessee, Governor Kerr Scott in North Carolina. But in 1950 the voters produced evidence of continued discontent by defeating the South's two most liberal senators—Frank P. Graham of North Carolina and Claude Pepper of Florida. Neither of the conservative victors, however, was of the Dixiecrat stripe.

As a viable organization the Dixiecrats were defunct. But, as Numan V. Bartley has said: "The Dixiecrat movement established the basic neobourbon nature of the reaction that was to play a central role in southern politics during the following decade. It fixed the broad aims and many of the programs that were to carry over into massive resistance" to school integration.[17] But at the onset of the 1950s the question was, "Whither Dixiecrats?" Was the movement a transitional step on the road to a new party affiliation, a two-party South? Or was it the beginning of a series of quadrennial efforts to choose independent electors who might prevent an electoral-college majority and win a new Compromise of 1877? Or was it a momentary defection after which the redneck masses would drift back into the party of Jefferson, Jackson, Bryan, and Roosevelt? It proved, in fact, to be all of these things.

As the election of 1952 approached, the quadrennial omens of rebellion reappeared.[18] By the time the Democratic convention met, six states had decided to determine their course of action only after the national convention: Texas, Louisiana, Mississippi, Georgia, South Carolina, and Virginia. The threat of a six-state rebellion raised questions suggested by the Dixiecrat rebellion four years before: Would the national ticket appear on the state ballots? (In 1948 it had been absent altogether from the Alabama ballot.) Would it appear under the Democratic label? And would the state parties support the ticket? The question came to be expressed in terms of party loyalty, accompanied by talk of loyalty pledges. The arrival of "loyalist" delegations from Texas and Mississippi and maneuvering for the presidential nomination further complicated the issue.

Supporters of the more liberal candidates, Averell Harriman of New York and Estes Kefauver of Tennessee, sought to challenge the southern conservatives with a loyalty pledge and thereby perhaps purge their opposition. Northern moderates, on the other hand, preferred to mollify the conservatives. In the end the moderates won passage of a resolution sponsored by Michigan's Senator Blair Moody which merely pledged delegates to use their influence to get the national ticket on the state ballot under the Democratic label. The convention adopted a moderate civil rights plank and nominated Adlai Stevenson of Illinois with John E. Sparkman of Alabama as his running mate. Party unifiers thus emerged victorious over the sectionalist liberals (some of whom wanted to slough off the former Dixiecrats), and the national ticket appeared under the Democratic label in every southern state.

The surface unity of the party, however, had merely papered over cracks that still existed under the surface. Three governors (James F. Byrnes of South Carolina, Robert F. Kennon of Louisiana, and Allan Shivers of Texas) endorsed Dwight D. Eisenhower, together with Dixiecrat Leander Perez of Louisiana; while Senator Harry Byrd of Virginia shortly before the election assumed a position of neutrality, as he had done in 1948 and would do again in later elections. In the end none of the Dixiecrat states went over to Eisenhower, although a significant Republican vote appeared in former Dixiecrat strongholds, but four states of the outer South did move out of the Democratic column: Florida, Tennessee, Texas, and Virginia.

The party dissensions continued to simmer during the next few years while the school segregation cases went up to the Supreme Court, and the Court ruled in May 1954 against segregation. Later that year J. Strom Thurmond staged a surprising political comeback when he won election to the senate on a write-in vote after the Democratic State Committee had refused to call a new primary upon the death of Burnet Maybank and chose its own nominee to fill the South Carolina vacancy.

But traditional forces that held the South to the Democratic party continued to operate: the mystique of party identification, a powerful if sometimes irrational force (perhaps *because* irrational); the power that seniority within the Democratic party gave to southern senators and representatives; the vested interest of the officeholding industry in the South, which might be damaged by the growth of an opposition party. Moreover, three other factors operated in the mid-fifties to discourage third-party adventures: no Democratic president provided a target for dissenters; Eisenhower avoided any personal linkage with the decision against segregation, and was so strongly favored that a split in the Democratic vote could not reasonably be expected to deadlock the electoral college; and at the state level the issue of segregation gave Democratic parties a new lease on life by reviving their traditional reason for being—by making them in most cases the agents of protest against desegregation.

An effort to muster a southern rebellion in 1956 once again failed despite the divisive currents that swept the

South after the school segregation decision. The decision itself had been followed by a period of relative calm, punctuated by the appearance of the citizens' councils in Mississippi. The implementation decision a year later, however, was followed by a mounting agitation in the region. In the spring of 1956 Senator Strom Thurmond sponsored the "Southern Manifesto" or "Declaration of Constitutional Principles," in which 101 southern members of Congress pronounced the Supreme Court's judgment "a clear abuse of judicial power." At about the same time the state of Virginia resurrected the doctrine of interposition and Senator Byrd proclaimed a policy of "massive resistance."[19]

Leaders of the national party, however, forestalled another loyalty battle in the 1956 convention. In 1953 the national committee had authorized a special advisory committee to study the rules: in 1955 that group brought in three proposals which the convention later adopted without dissent: (1) state parties in sending delegates undertook to assure an opportunity to vote for the nominees; (2) delegates certified by state parties were understood to be "bona fide Democrats" without a loyalty pledge; and (3) members of the national committee were required to declare affirmatively for the candidates on pain of expulsion. The convention endorsed civil rights in general terms but studiously avoided a direct endorsement of the desegregation decision.[20]

Against the odds a handful of intransigents again sought to revive the Dixiecrat alternative and ended with two splinter movements. In five southern states independent groups endorsed T. Coleman Andrews of Virginia, a right-wing opponent of the income tax. In Mississippi and South Carolina independents endorsed Senator Byrd, and only in those states did the independent tickets poll more than a negligible vote—29.4 percent in South Carolina and 17.3 percent in Mississippi. In both states they siphoned off the protest vote that had gone to Eisenhower four years earlier in black-belt counties and in silk-stocking wards of Charleston and Jackson. But few prominent Democrats associated themselves with either movement.[21]

In 1960 again the rumblings of rebellion failed to produce a major confrontation in the convention, partly because the resistance had waned (massive resistance had collapsed in Virginia and Arkansas the year before), partly because the southerners had a viable candidate in Lyndon Johnson, and partly because the Kennedy forces avoided antagonizing southerners with any action beyond a strong civil rights plank. During the campaign Johnson as candidate for vice president held most of the South in line by the lures and threats best portrayed in a fanciful story a newsman told James A. Michener. After expressing sympathy for the state leaders' problems with the platform, Kennedy's Catholicism, and the civil rights movement, "Good Ol' Lyndon" would remind them that if defeated he and Kennedy would remain in the Senate: ". . . and, Senator Buford and Senator Baxby, I just don't see how, if your defection is the cause of our defeat, you're ever going to get one little old bill through that Senate. Governor Beauregard, you say you have to have that new airport and you want to keep the Army base down here. How do you think you're going to get such bills through the Senate if Mr. Kennedy and I are sitting there solely because you didn't produce the vote that would have elected us?"[22]

The persistent plan for unpledged electors mostly failed again in 1960. In Alabama the spring primaries had placed six unpledged and five loyalist electors on the regular party ticket. In Mississippi an independent ticket won a plurality with 39 percent of the vote. The unpledged electors later cast their votes for Harry Byrd.

By 1964 Lyndon Johnson was president and the party was finally committed to the principle of racial equality—

and committed under the leadership of the first southern president since another Johnson from Tennessee. At the same time the Republican party under Barry Goldwater had reversed its role of a century before. In three conventions the Democratic party had warded off a repetition of the dramatic walkout in 1948. Disruption came from a different quarter in 1964. Among the events of that year it was a minor incident, but one fraught with emotion and with meaning for the party's future. A Mississippi delegation representing the predominantly black Freedom Democratic party demanded to be recognized in place of the traditional party which had systematically excluded blacks. After a moving plea from Mrs. Fannie Lou Hamer, who told about the beating and humiliation she had suffered after trying to register as a voter, the convention adopted a compromise proposal: no Mississippian would be seated without a pledge to support the party ticket; two members of the MFDP would sit in the convention; and no future convention would seat delegates from state parties which excluded citizens from participation by reason of race or color.[23]

The import of that decision was little diminished by the victors' refusal to recognize their victory or by their demonstration of protest against the decision. Four years later, in 1968, delegates of the Loyal National Democrats of Mississippi (twenty-two whites and twenty-two Negroes) took seats as the duly recognized representatives of Mississippi Democrats, along with delegates in similar groups from Alabama and Georgia, admitted jointly with those regular delegates who pledged not to oppose the party's nominees.

In 1964 three southern states had included Negroes in their delegations—Tennessee, North Carolina, and Georgia. In 1968 every single one included Negroes, without exception. It was thirty-two years since Cotton Ed Smith had bolted, twenty years since Hubert Humphrey had demanded the strong civil rights plank which provoked the Dixiecrat walkout. The 1968 convention, moreover, resolved in favor of measures to assure that "delegates [to future conventions] have been selected through a process in which all Democratic voters have had full and timely opportunity to participate."[24]

For more than twenty years the Democratic party has suffered a persistent erosion in its traditional base, the white voters. "I'm leaving the Democratic party," said a North Carolinian in 1968, "because I'm tired of higher taxes, inflation, socialism, dictatorship, lawlessness, wars, and rotten, stinking politics."[25] On the other hand the party has enjoyed a gradual accretion of black voters, a heavy accretion after passage of the Voting Rights Act of 1965. Some kind of transformation has already occurred when we can find a report to the *New York Times* describing the South Carolina Democratic party as "a close alliance among white moderates, courthouse politicians and blacks."[26] After the 1970 elections there were 665 black elected officials in eleven southern states. Some 3.3 million black voters out of a potential 5 million had been registered, and in more than one statewide election the black vote already had been the balance of power, mainly though not always on the Democratic side.[27] In 1964, for instance, black voters probably had supplied the decisive margin for Johnson in Arkansas, Florida, Tennessee, and Virginia. And early in 1971 southern governors one after another fell in line behind Georgia's Jimmy Carter to affirm that "the day of racial discrimination is over. . . ."[28]

The assumption by Kevin Phillips and others that the increase of black Democrats will drive white Democrats into the Republican party has yet to be proven, and it may be questioned not only in the light of recent experience but also of the late nineteenth century when Republicans, Populists, and Democrats alike cultivated Negro voters and reached understandings with Negro leaders. In 1964, by which time presidential Republicanism had begun to spill over into state and local elections, a reporter in Virginia remarked that it "was a delectable sight to see the old organization boys and the scions of the gentry out beating the bushes for poor-white and Negro votes."[29] Even the phenomenon of George Wallace's candidacy may cast some doubt on the Phillips assumption. Despite the flurry of excitement over northern "backlash" which accompanied Wallace's forays into the presidential primaries of 1964 and the fears of an electoral stalemate which accompanied his independent race in 1968, the Wallace movement ended as just another of those southern independent movements which have appeared and reappeared since 1936 without creating a deadlock. Wallace, like the "Jeffersonian Democrats" and "Texas Regulars" and unpledged electors of other years, offered Democrats an opportunity to protest against their national party without going over to the Republicans. And Wallace is now again the Democratic governor of Alabama.

The political changes that have swept the South since World War II are but a part of, and a result of, countless other changes wrought in the twentieth century by technology, industry, and urbanization. Countless old landmarks have disappeared: the one-crop agriculture and the one-crop industry, the white primary, the poll tax, the separate but equal doctrine, and the Solid South. In fact so many of the foundations of the old order in the New South have disappeared that we find ourselves in a new era, a post-New South that does not yet have a name. If the reason for the Solid South was Reconstruction, that has receded into the distant past and the region has experienced a Second Reconstruction which reached its climax under the leadership of a southern Democratic president. The region has finally moved out of the old Civil War-Reconstruction configurations in politics.

The most remarkable thing in these changes is perhaps not so much the death of the Solid South as the survival of the Democratic party, the tenacity of Democratic loyalties, the avoidance of another dramatic sectional split like that which divided the party in 1860 and opened the way to the election of Lincoln. Somehow along the way the Democrats escaped a shattering breakup on such a scale. The process that began as disruption in the 1940s, therefore, shows at least premonitory signs of ending as transformation and revival in the 1970s.

THREE

Toward a Party System

POLITICS IN THE SOUTH HAVE MOVED A LONG WAY SINCE 1902, when a leading Democratic paper referred to a Southern Republican convention as "the semi-annual gathering of the Federal pie brigade," and the delegates as "mossbacks," "revenue doodles," and "bung smellers," or since 1924 when South Carolina's Senator Coleman L. Blease noted that Calvin Coolidge got 1100 votes in his state: "I do not know where he got them" Blease said. "I was astonished to know that they were cast and shocked to know that they were counted."[1] As late as 1952 Alexander Heard could write in his book, *A Two-Party South?*, which was a timely and discerning prognosis of changes to come: "To many citizens of the South, a Republican is a curiosity. They may have heard about the Negro undertaker who goes to Republican conventions, or the eccentric railroad official who came from Ohio; but a genuine, breathing Republican is a rarity in most of the counties of the region."[2]

To categorize the Republicans of that time may seem at first an exercise in hair-splitting, but several distinctive types existed. Traditional GOP strength centered in the Blue Ridge and Smoky Mountains, "the great spine of Republicanism which runs down the back of the South,"[3] where stubborn Unionists had passed the faith on to succeeding generations. In three states (Virginia, Tennessee, and North Carolina) Republicans contested enough elec-

47

tions to deserve the name of a political party—and to give their adversaries more the character of a party than in the deep South where Democrats seldom faced an effective opposition. Less numerous but likewise heirs to a Civil War and Reconstruction tradition were the Negroes still loyal to the party of the Great Emancipator. By 1950 they were mostly older people; younger blacks had begun to desert Lincoln for Roosevelt and Truman. Along the way the Republicans had acquired a few recruits: old Populists who never rejoined the Democrats, immigrants from the North, businessmen who disliked New Deal economic policies, and a sprinkling of people who took umbrage at changing racial policies.

For more than half a century Dixie Republicans assumed a mood of defeatism that left a focus on presidential elections and federal jobs. State and local affairs they conceded to the Democrats, except in the mountains. For the professional "post office" Republicans, however, the New Deal years brought the worst political famine since the Civil War —twenty long years without a Republican president to make appointments. During that period V. O. Key and his associates in preparing the classic *Southern Politics* (1949) discovered that in the top leadership the old-time patronage referees were yielding to businessmen who often regarded the party as an expensive hobby but sometimes voiced the exuberant thought that they might contest elections. Most of the members, however, continued to be (as a Georgia Republican put it) a riff-raff interested only in federal appointments and in keeping down the number of deserving Republicans.[4]

Small as they were, these tiny groups were often wracked by factional wars, for the potential stakes in federal jobs could be great. To trace out all the Byzantine intrigues of factional struggle would require more time and patience than we can summon here. The internal struggles may be fairly said to have started in the Reconstruction period out of tensions among the carpetbag, Negro, and scalawag divisions of the party. Before the 1890s the hostilities began to assume the character of struggles between the "black and tans" and the "lily whites," terms which were common currency by that time if misleading, since the lily whites often included token Negroes and the black and tans usually included some whites. These factions rose and fell, with the long-term trend toward the lily-whites. By mid-century Mississippi remained the only state with an old-time black and tan organization that was recognized by the national party. But in 1956 "The Mississippi Black and Tan Grand Old Party," long led by black lawyer Perry Howard, had to share convention seats with a lily-white faction and in 1960 lost out altogether.[5] The South Carolina group once led by "Tieless Joe" Tolbert had been ousted twenty years before. Factional fights repeatedly went to the national conventions for decision, and chances of recognition often depended on a group's foresight in choosing the right presidential candidate. On two occasions during the twentieth century the choice of a presidential candidate turned on contests between these rival factions—in 1912 when William Howard Taft carried the convention against Theodore Roosevelt and forty years later, in 1952, when Taft's son Robert lost out to Dwight D. Eisenhower.

The election of 1952 marked a turning point in Republican fortunes, the beginning of a southern Republicanism that would contest elections, first at the presidential level, then at state and local levels, evolving gradually into a credible opposition party everywhere except the inner core of the deep South—and even there sporadically. The candidacy of the "nonpolitical" Eisenhower in 1952 first made it respectable, even modish, to vote Republican in the South. During the preconvention campaign an outpouring of popular enthusiasm for the general placed a sudden strain on the existing Republican organizations. Every southern delegation registered some support for Eisenhower except those from Tennessee and Mississippi, where party regulars dominated the organization and stood with Robert Taft, "Mr. Republican." The Eisenhower drive, however, fostered the illusion of a transformation more sudden than actually occurred. The impression of a popular tide overwhelming the entrenched bosses arose from what appears in another perspective to have been a battle between existing factions, with the "outs" recruiting Eisenhower supporters and charging "manipulation" and "theft" against the "ins" who controlled the national committee and favored Taft supporters over rival delegates.

The crucial battles involved contesting delegations from Georgia, Louisiana, and Texas. In each case, however, the contestants represented groups that had sought recognition before 1952.[6] In Georgia the "Tucker faction" and the "Foster faction" had functioned as separate Republican parties with separate officers and separate delegations. The Tucker group, which had been seated in 1944 and 1948, went for Eisenhower. In Louisiana the general's forces were led by John Minor Wisdom, a New Orleans lawyer who represented a business-professional influx into the party and who had struggled in the 1940s against the entrenched leaders. In New Orleans Wisdom mobilized fresh recruits to invade the Republican meetings, but Old Guard control of the state machinery forced his adherents into a rump convention.

In Texas the battle assumed larger proportions. There the party organization had been controlled for years by R. B. Creager, a Taft man. After Creager's death in 1950 Henry Zweifel of Fort Worth won the position of national committeeman over J. H. (Jack) Porter of Houston. Two years later the Porter faction found in Eisenhower a personality around whom it could rally dissatisfied Democrats and independents to seize control from the Old Guard. Organized by the Eisenhower-for-President Club of Texas, the opposition exploited ambiguities in the Texas laws to swamp precinct and county meetings with new members. The result was an overwhelming victory which the Zweifel forces nullified by deciding contests in favor of rump sessions that named Taft delegates. The Porter-Eisenhower faction then held a separate state convention, which was much the better attended, and named a separate delegation.

Both groups comprised mainly business and professional men, but some measure of difference may be derived from Zweifel's claims that Eisenhower was backed by the Communist *Daily Worker*, that "majority rule is not always right," and that his group had saved the party from "mob rule." Zweifel thus made himself the perfect butt for charges of a "raw deal" and a "steal," although some merit must be conceded to his claim that the party had been invaded by Democrats. The convention vote on the Georgia, Louisiana, and Texas contests focused attention on southern Republicanism, and the seating of the Eisenhower delegates gave recognition to groups that had a broader public appeal and had most of the eager beavers who wanted to contest elections.

In the canvass that followed, Eisenhower campaigned more widely in the South than any previous Republican candidate. On September 2, 1952, he left for a tour that carried him to Atlanta, Jacksonville, and Miami and the next day to Tampa, Birmingham, and Little Rock, with large and enthusiastic crowds in each. In Columbia, South Carolina, he appeared on the state house steps with Governor James F. Byrnes. When the band struck up "Dixie," Eisenhower leaped from his chair and shouted to the crowd: "I always stand up when they play that song." Except for a few such gestures to local sentiment, however, he avoided appeals on strictly sectional grounds and endorsed equal rights for all citizens in several southern speeches. Altogether Eisenhower visited nine southern states, and Adlai Stevenson visited four. Never again would presidential candidates of either party take the South for granted.[7]

Eisenhower carried four of the former Confederate states —Florida, Tennessee, Texas and Virginia; but significantly these were states outside the deep South, where the Democrats had pacified the Dixiecrat rebels enough to restore a degree of party regularity.[8] Traditionally the Republican vote peaked at high altitudes, and in the mountain strongholds Eisenhower overwhelmed Stevenson. In states with mountain areas the top quartile of Eisenhower counties generally had stood in the top quartile for Hoover in 1928 and Dewey in 1948. But an avalanche of Republican votes swept down the mountainsides into the foothill cities and on beyond into the flatland black belts. There the Dixiecrats of 1948 had loosened the inhibitions against bolting the Democrats, and the candidacy of a "nonpolitical" hero further eased the reluctance to vote Republican. In 1952 the Republican ticket, or tickets of Independents for Eisenhower in Mississippi and South Carolina, offered the only vehicle for a protest vote against the national Democrats.

More propitious for a durable Republicanism, however, was the urban vote. In the cities a leaning toward middle-class Republicanism had manifested itself sporadically even before the turn of the century, again in the Taft vote of 1908, and again in the 1920s. In 1952 middle-class Republicanism began to take on great proportions. To some extent it represented an issue vote against Democratic policies; to some extent in 1952 and increasingly in subsequent elections, a status vote. Republicanism became the style, and a fashion of "conservative chic" swept through the white suburbs. Checks of urban precincts repeatedly showed a correlation between high income and Republican voting. The most overwhelmingly Republican were the upper-income white residential areas. The areas most heavily for Adlai Stevenson were the black precincts and, to a lesser degree, the low-income white precincts. Political scientist Donald Strong made such findings in Little Rock, Jacksonville, Atlanta, Charlotte, Charleston, Memphis, Richmond, Houston, Dallas, Mobile, and Birmingham.

The phenomenon of urban Republicanism, viewed from a different angle, assumed even greater significance when Strong singled out those areas in which the Democratic vote had declined most sharply from the peak year of 1936. The counties of greatest loss in the deep South (Alabama, Louisiana, Mississippi, South Carolina) and in Tennessee and Virginia were in the top quartile of proportionate Negro population, counties where the voters (mostly white) were most alarmed by the Truman racial policies. In the same states plus Arkansas and North Carolina an overlap of support for Thurmond and Eisenhower suggested a Dixiecrat-to-Republican trend. But the most consistent pattern of gain for the Republicans occurred in the cities. In each of the former Confederate states the counties with larger cities appeared among the counties of heaviest Democratic loss. South Carolina was the one exception, but only because a heavy Republican vote in the rural black belt overshadowed the urban vote. Even there Eisenhower was strong in Charleston and in up-country towns such as Columbia and Greenville.

Similar patterns prevailed four years later. In 1956 Eisenhower carried the same four southern states plus Louisiana. Again he ran well in the cities, especially in the upper-income neighborhoods, and he showed a greater gain over the 1936 vote in cities than in the non-urban counties. The importance of his urban vote was further emphasized by the failure to hold gains among whites in the black belts. The race issue had entered a new phase after the 1954 decision against school segregation. The president had done nothing to associate himself with the decision, calculatedly refused to endorse it, and on at least one occasion privately expressed disagreement with it; but he had appointed the chief justice who wrote the opinion. Eisenhower was inhibited against vigorous executive action by a philosophy which favored local government and by a personal conviction that one could not change man's hearts by law. In areas of federal authority, however, he continued the Truman policy of integrating the military and civil services, and he undertook to desegregate public facilities in Washington. He no longer offered the same outlet for segregationist protest, and his vote dropped in the black-belts, particularly in those of South Carolina and Mississippi, where independent slates gave outlets for white intransigents. On the other hand Eisenhower divided the Negro vote with Stevenson to a greater degree than in 1952. Even in the deep South, at least in Georgia and Louisiana, moderate Republican organizations actively cultivated and mobilized black voters, whose numbers were already slowly increasing and who were disillusioned by the tendency of Stevenson to mollify segregationists.[9]

In three consecutive presidential elections the Solid South had split. In 1948 the Dixiecrats had broken off four states of the deep South; in 1952 Eisenhower carried four states of the outer South, and in 1956 he gained a fifth in the deep South—Louisiana. During Eisenhower's second term the resistance to desegregation edicts reached a climax in the politics of massive resistance. In 1957 the stand of Governor Orval Faubus against school desegregation in Arkansas forced the president to dispatch troops to Little Rock, with damaging effects on Republican politics in the South, but the Republican committee of Georgia, *mirabile dictu*, rose to the occasion with a resolution commending Eisenhower's action.[10] Further confrontations between state and presidential authority were avoided, but confrontations with the courts and disturbances in the streets continued to mount until Virginia abandoned massive resistance in 1959.

The Kennedy-Nixon election of 1960 tested the durability of the new presidential Republicanism. The ticket headed by Richard M. Nixon no longer carried the prestige of a military hero at the top, while the Democrats for the third time in succession named a southerner for vice president—Lyndon Johnson, who had a broader base of support in the region than either John Sparkman (1952) or Estes Kefauver (1956), and who campaigned vigorously through the South on a 2500-mile whistle-stop tour, giving sixty speeches along the way. John F. Kennedy visited six southern states, but Nixon made at least one stop in each southern state: in fact he launched his campaign in August with trips to Greensboro, North Carolina, to several stops in Alabama, and to Atlanta where his reception impressed Theodore H. White as a "Roman triumph." No Democratic candidate had campaigned in Georgia in a quarter century, Nixon declared in Atlanta. "I think it's time for the Democratic candidates for the Presidency to quit taking Georgia and the South for granted."[11]

Nixon lost Georgia, but held most of the Eisenhower gains and carried three of the Eisenhower states—Florida, Tennessee, and Virginia—but neither Texas nor Louisiana. Eisenhower had carried between 48 and 49 percent of the vote in the former Confederate states; Nixon in losing got about 46 percent. In metropolitan areas of the South, where Eisenhower had a majority, Nixon still had a plurality, and in the black belts and some cities of the deep South he improved on the general's record. The Negro vote, however, drifted back toward the Democrats.[12]

Through all of this the Republican phenomenon in the South was in its most solid gains and its most durable form an urban phenomenon. Cities have often been the incubators of change, less bound by tradition than smaller communities, more receptive to the new; and during the Eisenhower years the South had reached its urban breakthrough and ceased to be predominantly rural. After surveying the preferences of voters in 1952, political scientist Donald Strong exclaimed, "They're acting like Yankees!" In some part, at least, this was because they *were* Yankees, drawn South by economic opportunity like the carpetbaggers of old and then impelled into politics: executives and managers of industry and business, or government workers in the Washington suburbs, or retired residents of the sun belt—such men as industrialist Roger Milliken, financial angel of Republicanism in South Carolina, Virginia Republican chairman I. Lee Potter, or Alabama chairman Thomas Brigham, who came respectively from New York, Pennsylvania, and Vermont. And prosperous natives found their voting behavior "no longer being determined by consideration of one's great-grandfather's activities in the 1860s but rather by calculations of economic interest which are the same both North and South."[13]

Among the newcomers and natives alike a new type had appeared—the organization man, a worthy successor to Ralph McGill's "certain type, small town rich man." In 1961 Francis Pickens Miller, a liberal Democrat of Virginia and not an altogether sympathetic observer, wrote a provocative description:

> His appearance represents a complete break with the past. With rare exceptions there has never been anyone like him in the South before. He is the executive servant of the new industrial society. Heretofore the normal white Southerner has been no man's servant. He has served only his loyalties and his prejudices.
>
> Southerners in the past have generally been rooted persons. . . . But these organization men are for the most part rootless persons . . . , nomads who do not claim any locale as their permanent home. . . .

Because the Southern industrial development is still in its infancy and represents such a complete break with the past, these young men accurately reflect the values of the institutions and interests they serve. They show little evidence of having been influenced by what used to be called "Southern culture. . . ."

Men are seldom willing to admit that materialism is their philosophy of life, and that is true of these organization men. They prefer to take their stand on the higher ground of principle, and their principles are generally expressed in terms of free enterprise, fiscal sanity, states rights and racial integrity.

. . . They seem to me to be momentary men—individuals who have breadth, but no length or depth, men whose lives are like cross sections of history without reflecting any sense of continuity with the living stream of the past or with the living stream of the future. But they constitute the raw material out of which new political organizations in the South will be formed.[14]

But while southern voters might be acting like Yankees, southern cities were not acting like Yankee cities. In 1962 a reporter asked Senator Barry Goldwater to explain why Republicans did well in southern cities but lost rural areas while the reverse was true in the North. "I can't answer that," Goldwater replied.[15] A significant part of the answer, at least, derived from the lack of those features that made northern cities Democratic: the organized labor, immigrant, and black groups that had joined the New Deal coalition. The newer industry in the South was not for the most part a mass production industry. Plants were smaller, and in some areas more capital-intensive than in earlier southern industry, requiring a higher ratio of skilled, white collar, professional, and managerial personnel. Employment in manufacturing, in fact, was relatively smaller in southern cities. The New Dealers' hope to extend the northern coali-

tion of labor and minority voters into the South had found-
ered on the sectional and racial passions of the postwar
years, and the hope all but disappeared in the 1950s.

In 1952 and 1956 the Eisenhower campaigns afforded an
exaggerated case of presidential Republicanism. But the
southerner who sported a bumper sticker that said "I'm a
Democrat but I like Ike" represented a type that went back
as far as Reconstruction. In 1948 the last southern states to
require pledges of party loyalty from Democratic primary
voters had dropped the pledge for presidential races.[16] The
weight of traditional Democratic loyalties and vested interests, however, continued to hold back the rise of state and
local Republicanism. Yet the Republicans had some ad-
vantages besides the disruption of Democracy and the popularity of Eisenhower: among them were the nationalization
of southern politics with the spread of modern communi-
cations, the vulnerability of rusty Democratic organizations
that had never faced real opposition, and the opportunity
for ambitious young men to advance more quickly in the
Republican ranks.

At first, however, Republicans failed to exploit their
opportunity to the fullest advantage. During the 1950s they
added only five new southern congressmen while holding
the two traditionally Republican mountain districts of Tennessee. In either 1952 or 1954 they carried and held until
the end of the decade two seats in Virginia (the Washington suburbs and Roanoke) and one each in Florida (St.
Petersburg-Tampa), North Carolina (Charlotte plus an Ap-
palachian hinterland), and Texas (Dallas). In a total of 106
districts the largest number contested in the 1950s was 42,
and the number fell to 22 in 1958. Even some metropolitan
districts went by default; in 1952 three Louisiana Republicans withdrew from congressional races as a gesture to
Governor Kennon for his support of Eisenhower.[17]

The defeat of Nixon and the rise of John F. Kennedy

opened another new era in southern Republicanism. Once
again the target for discontent was a Democratic president,
and one who entered office just as the Negro revolt reached
a climax with the 1960 sit-ins, the 1961 freedom rides, the
1962 imbroglio at Ole Miss, the 1963 demonstrations at
Birmingham and the march on Washington. Kennedy
played a cautious game with the race issue, appointed as
judges southern Democrats who stood in some instances
to the right of Eisenhower appointees, and undertook no
significant legislative initiatives before 1963 when he endorsed the pending civil rights bill. Still his platform and
his rhetoric, more than Eisenhower's, committed him to
civil rights, and his office obligated him to enforce the laws
and court decisions. The cosmopolitanism of Kennedy was
more alien to the South than the personal style of Eisenhower, who was born in Texas and did much of his peace-
time service in the South. And where Eisenhower managed
to avoid direct confrontations except at Little Rock, Kennedy had one after another thrust upon him almost from
the beginning.

Mounting Kennedyphobia gave southern Republicans a
new opening to the right, and one that they were better pre-
pared to exploit than they had been a decade before. After
several years of neglected opportunity, the Republican National Committee in 1957 had created a Southern Division,
headed from then until 1966 by I. Lee Potter, Virginia's
Republican chairman and national committeeman. Beginning with a rally at Little Rock in June 1958, Potter undertook an active program of recruiting and publicity, made
dozens of speeches on the growth of southern Republicanism. He got the enthusiastic help of Arizona's Senator Barry
Goldwater, chairman of the Republican Senatorial Campaign Committee since 1954; and "Operation Dixie" became closely tied to the new conservatism that Goldwater
promoted.[18] In 1961 a clear portent of the emerging south-

ern strategy came when Goldwater, in the course of "poop-
ing around," told newsmen in Atlanta: "We're not going
to get the Negro vote as a bloc in 1964 and 1968, so we
ought to go hunting where the ducks are." Ironically Atlanta was one place where Nixon had got a majority of
Negro vote—nearly 60 percent.[19]

In May 1961 the victory of John Tower in a special election to fill Lyndon Johnson's vacated seat in the senate
spurred new hope among southern Republicans. Other
signs of grassroots strength followed—a Republican mayor
in Mobile, two Republican aldermen in Atlanta, two Republican legislators in South Carolina. In 1962 Republican senatorial candidates made serious challenges in South
Carolina and Louisiana. In Alabama pro-Goldwater in-
surgents captured the state convention, named 32-year-old
John Grenier their chairman, and nominated for the senate James D. Martin, who called for "a return to the spirit
of '61—1861, when our fathers formed a new nation. . . .
The South has risen!" Martin, who scored dramatic gains
among white voters in the black belt, came within six thou-
sand votes of unseating Lister Hill. At the same time Texas
Republican Jack Cox won over 46 percent of the vote for
governor. In congressional races the party added four members from the South, for a total of eleven. By 1963 Republican legislators, councilmen, and mayors were popping up
all across the South. In Mississippi a Republican gubernatorial campaign gathered 39 percent of the vote for Rubel
Phillips, whose slogan was "ko the Kennedys."[20]

Meanwhile a Goldwater boom was gathering force. The
movement to nominate Barry Goldwater was the first Republican campaign to have its inception in the South since
1895, when Mark Hanna took up residence at Thomasville,
Georgia, to cultivate support for William McKinley. In
1959 the South Carolina Republican chairman Gregory D.
Shorey, Jr., brought Goldwater to Greenville to speak at a

dinner. There and on statewide television Shorey touted Goldwater as a presidential candidate. In March 1960, after Goldwater addressed the state convention, South Carolina Republicans pledged their delegates to support him at the national convention. There the senator was placed in nomination mainly so that he could expound his philosophy in a withdrawal speech and, incidentally, urge his followers to stay within the party: "Let's grow up, conservatives! If we want to take this party back, and I think we can some day, let's go to work!" In the campaign Goldwater worked loyally for the Nixon ticket.[21]

By the fall of 1961 F. Clifton White of New York had formed the nucleus of a movement to draft Goldwater. With the help of John Ashbrooke, an Ohio congressman, and William A. Rusher, publisher of the conservative *National Review*, White quietly cultivated party leaders while Goldwater continued his work with the Senate Republican Campaign Committee, with special attention to the South. Republican gains in southern state and local elections gave impetus to the "southern strategy" which the Goldwater group soon unfolded. In December 1962, at a meeting in Chicago, White unveiled a map which suggested that Goldwater could carry the South and "heartland" states of the Midwest. These, together with other states won by Nixon, would more than carry him over the top. Early in 1963 the proposed strategy began to appear in newspaper and periodical stories, the first of which William Rusher printed in *National Review* for February 12 under the title "Crossroads for the GOP."[22]

Reviewing the economic and social forces which since Word War II had eroded the one-party South, and the statistics of Republican growth, Rusher cited an unnamed southern senator who predicted that Goldwater could sweep 165 southern and border-state electoral votes against Kennedy. Against charges of racism which already had been leveled at Potter's Operation Dixie, Rusher argued that southern Republicans were less firmly committed to segregation than southern Democrats: "the Republican Party is strongest in the southern cities and suburbs, where the tides of social change are tending to run fastest. It was the primitive wool-hats of the Alabama backwoods who saved Lister Hill for John Kennedy." But Rusher failed to account for the surge of Republican votes from whites in the black belt.

In April 1963 the National Draft Goldwater Committee went public with Texas Republican Chairman Peter O'Donnell as chairman and *U. S. News and World Report* blossomed out with a projected 1964 political map bearing a close resemblance to Clifton White's, which itself soon appeared in a "Draft Goldwater" pamphlet. Maps much like these appeared later in Kevin Phillips' *Emerging Republican Majority*.

In November 1963 the tragedy at Dallas drastically altered the aspect of the campaign. Instead of Kennedy the Republicans would face a southern president who would gain support from reaction to the assassination. Lyndon Johnson was indeed able to reassure many southerners by his origins and his style. One perhaps apocryphal Texas lady was said to have expressed comfort that, at last, the country had a president who spoke without an accent.[23] But the Goldwater campaign had developed a life of its own, despite the genuine reluctance of the candidate, and the major challengers had been severely weakened—Nixon by his losing race for governor of California in 1962, Rockefeller by his divorce and remarriage in 1963.

In the South the Goldwater movement captured nearly every delegate before the convention opened. Between 1960 and 1964 the right-wing movement which Goldwater represented altered the party's character in the southern states, in some cases by a dramatic sudden overturn. In Georgia, for instance, the Goldwater drive ousted Robert Snodgrass, national committeeman from 1952 to 1964, who had fostered a moderate party which made successful appeals to Negro voters in Atlanta. To take his place the Goldwaterites brought back Roscoe Pickett, Jr., once leader of the Taft wing and son of an old-time southern Republican leader. The state sent its first all-white delegation to the national convention in 1964. So did Tennessee.[24] "The young men who directed this seizure," wrote Theodore H. White, were "almost all of a kind—men between thirty and forty years old, city people, well-bred, moderate segregationists, efficient, more at ease at suburban cocktail parties than when whiskey-belting in courthouse chambers. One could start with almost any of them—Peter O'Donnell of Texas, Wirt Yerger of Mississippi, Drake Edens of South Carolina, or John Grenier of Alabama." O'Donnell became chairman of the Draft Goldwater Committee; Grenier directed the effort to win southern delegates and later served as executive secretary of the Republican National Committee. White's description carries some hint of polish and breeding, but a report by newsman Robert D. Novak suggested something else. At a session in Denver during the Republican National Committee meeting in June, 1963, Novak reported that two unnamed southern state chairmen engaged in a boisterous conversation about "nigger-lovers" while black waiters served lunch.[25]

The course of events, the character of Goldwater supporters in the deep South, and the candidate's actions conspired to stamp Goldwater the segregationist candidate. Goldwater had refused, on constitutional principle, to vote for the Civil Rights Act of 1964; and although the principle was not segregation, many identified him with that cause, not altogether without reason. During the campaign Goldwater got the support of Senator J. Strom Thurmond, the greatest Dixiecrat of them all, who not only endorsed Goldwater (as he had endorsed Nixon in 1960) but announced his own switch to what he called the "Goldwater Republican party." Near the end of the campaign Goldwater appeared on a platform in Columbia with Thurmond and other segregationists for a speech televised throughout the Confederacy.[26]

Goldwater's southern strategy proved in the end an effective plan only for the convention, where Grenier delivered 271 out of 278 southern votes, but a poor plan for the election, even in the South. By rejecting the new black voters and neglecting the moderate middle class, by a series of gaffes which made him seem impulsive, even trigger-happy, and hostile to farm programs, social security, and TVA, Goldwater left himself only one center of strength outside Arizona—the Dixiecrat belt where race still prevailed as the central theme of southern politics.[27]

In winning the four Dixiecrat states plus Georgia, states which had never gone Republican since Reconstruction, Goldwater took the core of the old Solid South, but he lost the rest of the region. In the South as a whole he got a smaller percentage of the vote than either Eisenhower or Nixon, and with his five states a smaller electoral vote than Eisenhower. The pattern, indeed, almost perfectly reversed the Eisenhower pattern. Goldwater did best in the black belts, worst in the cities; gained ground in the non-metropolitan South, lost ground in the mountains. In the deep South, political scientist Bernard Cosman found, the Republican politics of race and sectionalism in 1964 almost erased class patterns in voting—voters at all economic levels were intoxicated with Goldwater. In the outer South, where race assumed less salience as an issue, the vote followed more nearly the class lines of Eisenhower's vote, but Goldwater's image as an extremist frightened voters much as it did in the rest of the country, and he lost all the Eisenhower-Nixon states.

If 1964 should be a Democratic year, William Rusher had

asked in 1963: "How can the Republican convention, then, best build for a successful future? By turning its back on the new, conservative and increasingly Republican South and gumming blintzes with Nelson Rockefeller? Or by nominating a candidate who—win or lose—will galvanize the party in a vast new area, carry fresh scores and perhaps hundreds of southern Republicans to unprecedented local victories, and lay the foundations for a truly national Republican Party, ready to fight and win in 1968 and all the years beyond?"[28] The question remained, and remains today, whether Goldwater performed in the deep South a role like that Al Smith once performed in the Northeast, where he helped bring urban labor and ethnic groups over to the Democratic party, even while losing. The answer cannot emerge fully until the phenomenon of George Wallace has run its course, but the gain so far seems highly unstable. Instead of building on the urban foundation of Republican growth, Goldwater courted the white diehards of the black belts whom William G. Carleton called "an alienated people . . . bypassed by the nation's history," like the Jacobites of eighteenth-century Scotland or the Royalists of nineteenth-century France.[29] These voters have proven to be the most volatile element in southern politics, swept into different camps by the winds of passion—from Thurmond to Eisenhower to independent electors to Goldwater to Wallace—seeming often to care more for the catharsis of "showing them how we feel" than for political victory.

In 1964 southern Republicans netted five new congressional seats for a total of sixteen. They gained seven in the deep South (five in Alabama and one each in Georgia and Mississippi) but lost two in Texas. In 1965 they gained yet another when South Carolina's Albert Watson returned as a Republican after resigning in protest against his loss of Democratic seniority for supporting Goldwater. In 1966 Republicans increased the number of their southern congressmen yet again—to twenty-three—but that occurred even while they were losing three of the deep South seats (two in Alabama, one in Mississippi) which had come in with the Goldwater tide. Gains occurred, not in the Goldwater states (except one in Georgia), but in each of the other southern states.[30]

After Goldwater southern Republicans offered an engrossing study in contrasts. A month after the 1964 elections Robert Gavin, the losing candidate for governor of North Carolina, told Republican governors in Denver that he would "never again" go along with the so-called southern strategy. "I don't want this party to be racist or a lily-white party. The quicker we admit that Negroes have a right to vote and are going to vote, the better it will be for us." The next year Virginia's A. Linwood Holton as Republican candidate for governor made a wide ranging appeal that embraced Negro and union voters. Indeed Virginia's Republicans had often taken a more liberal stance than the Democrats under Harry Byrd, but Negroes, still shy from the Goldwater campaign, probably gave the Democrats the winning margin.[31] In 1969, however, Holton would become the first Republican elected governor since Reconstruction.

In 1966 Tennessee's Howard Baker won election as a Republican senator after making a vigorous appeal for the support of black voters, and Republican Winthrop Rockefeller defeated a blatant race baiter in the race for governor of Arkansas. Yet at the same time Claude Kirk was elected governor of Florida with the slogan "Your home is your castle—protect it"—a phrase designed to exploit racial feeling. And in South Carolina Strom Thurmond's followers seized control of the party in a convention that met underneath a gigantic Confederate flag.[32]

The results of gubernatorial and congressional races in Alabama, Georgia, and Mississippi, however, cast some doubt on Republican ability to "outsegregate" Democrats in the deep South, to win (as an Alabama newsman put it) by trying "to cut a chaw off the same ol' plug—racism—the Democrats have been chewin' on for decades."[33] In Alabama John Grenier urged the party to turn around and form a coalition of city voters, middle-income whites in rural areas, and at least 30 percent of the blacks. In 1964 Grenier had decided to go with Goldwater, he said, in a deliberate ploy to "break the black belt where the whites automatically voted Democratic. . . . You couldn't jar those people loose from the Democrats without somebody they *thought* was a segregationist." In 1968 Grenier found that he could not regain the state chairmanship—control had shifted to the very people he had jarred loose. Like other Frankensteins, Robert Sherrill wrote, he had lost control of the monster.[34]

Thus, in general, the old pattern of contrast between deep South and outer South reappeared in the makeup of the Republican party, and corresponded roughly to the contrast between the Eisenhower and Goldwater Republicans, the new Republicans of the 1950s and the new Republicans of the 1960s.

The rise of the Republican right in the deep South introduced a new element into the calculations of party leaders. As the confused and riotous and tragic spectacle of politics unfolded in 1968, the winning candidate incurred a heavy obligation to the southern right wingers, including the chief Dixiecrat-become-Republican, J. Strom Thurmond himself, who assumed the role of kingmaker in his first Republican convention. The most telling version of southern strategy in 1968 was perhaps the preconvention strategy of southern Republican state chairmen. This group, if it had forgotten nothing, had at least learned something from the 1964 disaster—that a dogmatic conservative cannot win. Their strategy, as described by the British reporters who wrote *An American Melodrama: The Presidential Cam-*

paign of 1968, was one of "hanging loose" to insure that the winning candidate would have to sweat a little first. Their secret weapon was California's Governor Ronald Reagan.[35]

Richard Nixon had won their acceptance, if not their enthusiasm, by staying regular, working for the ticket in 1964, and doing sundry favors afterward. The strategy very nearly backfired when southern delegates, picking up the scent of a Reagan movement, began to strain at the leash held by their leaders, but the strategy succeeded brilliantly when Thurmond stepped forward to prevent the erosion of Nixon's southern support. Thurmond himself had been committed to Nixon since a conference with the candidate in Atlanta on June 1, at which Nixon's support of the antiballistic missile system seemed to be the clincher. Whatever the specifics of their understanding, Richard Nixon owed his nomination in a significant measure to Thurmond. And even more so did Spiro Agnew.[36]

The southern strategy for the postconvention campaign was largely dictated by the apparent threat from George Wallace who ended with more of an extremist image than Goldwater and, like Goldwater, carried only the deep South. But Richard Nixon, moving from his position in the Republican center, deliberately reached toward the right rather than toward the left in his statements on busing, guidelines, and law and order, all of which could be interpreted as oblique hints to the segregationists.

The electoral map of 1968 seemed at first startlingly different from any that went before. Most startling, of course, was that the Democratic candidate carried only one state of the old Confederacy, Texas, ran second to Nixon in Florida and Virginia, second to Wallace in Alabama, Louisiana, and Mississippi, and third in the other five states and the region as a whole. But at a second look the electoral map of 1968 becomes a composite of earlier maps, registering both the old Dixiecrat South and the new Republican

South. Wallace had the former minus South Carolina plus Georgia and Arkansas. And Nixon had the three states he had carried in 1960, Florida, Tennessee, and Virginia plus the two Carolinas, and none of them with a majority. Indeed he ended with a smaller proportion of the southern vote than he or Eisenhower or Goldwater had polled earlier.

In some ways recent Republican strategies, like the electoral maps, seemed startlingly different from anything that went before, but a second look reveals striking parallels to the post-Reconstruction period. Hayes pursued Whiggish southerners; Eisenhower and Nixon scored with their modern counterparts in suburban elephant jungles like Charlotte's Myers Park. Garfield, Arthur, and Harrison pursued agrarian rebels; Goldwater scored with segregationist rebels. Hayes and his successors did not exactly pursue black voters, but expected to hold their vote; Eisenhower in 1956 and Nixon in 1960 scored among black voters, even while sweeping the silk-stocking precincts. Barry Goldwater was the first Republican candidate to spurn the Negro vote.

Ambiguities in the southern strategy of Nixon have paralleled ambiguities in the strategy of Hayes and his successors. Therein lies an enduring Republican problem, vacillation between appeasement of southern sensitivities and impatience with southern intransigence. The fatal result has been the failure to convey a sense of conviction, from Hayes to Nixon. "Southern Republicans must not climb aboard the sinking ship of racial injustice," Nixon told a party meeting at Jackson, Mississippi, in 1966. "They should let the Southern Democrats sink with it, as they have sailed with it."[37] Yet from 1968 to 1970 Nixon and members of his entourage issued contradictory statements about guidelines for desegregation, busing for integration, voting rights, and other issues related to racial discrimination.

The signals to white intransigents in such statements, in nominations to the Supreme Court, in the bitter appeal to sectionalism after the Carswell defeat, and in the unleashing of Spiro Agnew had all clashed with measures to ease and enforce court-ordered desegregation and with proposals to reform the welfare system in ways that would benefit most of all southern Negroes. The message that came through conveyed at best a conflict of purpose and at worst an artless deceit.

The midterm elections of 1970 registered a setback for the southern strategy except in Tennessee, where Republicans defeated Senator Albert Gore and elected a governor. Even there the GOP lost its precarious control in the lower house of the legislature. Republicans managed to hold their twenty-six congressional seats and even to add one in Virginia, but lost governorships in Arkansas and Florida and failed in all other statewide elections across the South. "Southerners," a report to the liberal Republican Ripon Society observed, "appeared to be recognizing the administration's demagoguery on the race issue, on law and order, and on the Haynsworth and Carswell nominations as a continuation of the cynical attempts by corporate interests, largely Northern, to distract them from the social and economic issues that affect their lives. And though these appeals were unfailingly couched in terms of sympathy for the South, the voters also began to see them as an indication of contempt for all Southerners, black and white alike."[38]

To project the political future from the 1970 elections, however, might be as erroneous as to project the future from 1964 or 1968. The drift of southern politics will depend largely upon the two different groups of people who have felt most aggrieved at the policies of the recent past: some five million Wallace voters and some three million (potentially five million) black voters, whose counterparts, the independents and freedmen of the nineteenth century, also figured as the objects of southern strategy. If any party can achieve the political ambidexterity to bring substantial numbers of both groups under one tent, that party can not only gain an advantage but can do much at the same time to advance the cause of reconciliation.

The Democrats may have the better chance. Enough has been revealed by current pundits and pollsters about the tug between voting one's prejudices and voting one's pocketbook to suggest that among Wallacites, aside from the dogmatic true believers, Democratic loyalties die hard. Southern strategists can find a sobering truth in the observation of a South Carolinian on the Republican vote during the 1960s: "There ain't that many Republicans in South Carolina, just a lot of mad Democrats."[39] In trying to reach "mad Democrats," Republicans will have to work against their twentieth-century image as the party of Depression (if no longer of Reconstruction), as what a Democratic circular in Mississippi a few years ago called "a silk-stocking type that hold Coca-Cola and coffee drinking parties in the big house on the hill."[40]

Republicans, despite their recent history, may find it easier to revive the traditional support of black southerners. It is hard to believe that black voters, whose numbers are increasing, can much longer be neglected by the party which was their traditional home before Franklin Roosevelt, which today has the only Negro senator, which polled a sizeable black vote for its presidential candidates in 1956 and 1960 and, even after Goldwater, for its gubernatorial candidates in Arkansas, Tennessee, and Virginia. After the 1970 elections the signs began to appear that Republicans were moving away from the southern strategy of Goldwater and back toward the southern strategy of Hayes, the most spectacular case in point being Senator Thurmond's appointment of a black assistant. The need for votes in party battles will of necessity invite appeals to black voters by both parties, and such a development might finally vindicate the belief of Rutherford Hayes that a political division in the white

South would provide the best guarantee of civil rights for the black South.

Whatever may be the future direction of voting or the future resolution of issues, one fundamental development appears in a review of the past two decades: the emergence of a party system, which has opened the politics of the South to a range of possibility that would have seemed unthinkable just twenty years ago. In one of his last books Richard Hofstadter argued that the idea of a party system, the idea that a loyal opposition has the right to exist, first became established in the early years of the Republic and constituted one of the original American contributions to the art of politics.[41] In the one-party South, however, this idea never became institutionalized before the mid-twentieth century. Yet since 1952 the Republican party has created a viable opposition for the first time since the brief heyday of the Whigs in the 1840s. The two-party system, therefore, has approached nationwide scope for the first time in more than a century, a development which may once again confound the soothsayers, who are currently hag-ridden by symptoms of fragmentation in the body politic.

Bibliographical Note

THE BEST STARTING POINT FOR A STUDY OF SOUTHERN POLITICS
is Dewey W. Grantham, Jr.'s *The Democratic South* (Athens: University of Georgia Press, 1963), the Eugenia Dorothy Blount Lamar Memorial Lectures for 1962, in which
Grantham covers southern politics since the Civil War with
remarkable comprehensiveness in fewer than a hundred
pages. Other general works that give broad coverage in-
clude Paul Lewinson, *Race, Class, and Party* (New York:
Oxford University Press, 1932); C. Vann Woodward, *Origins of the New South, 1877–1913* (Baton Rouge: Louisiana
State University Press, 1951); and George B. Tindall, *The
Emergence of the New South, 1913–1945* (Baton Rouge:
Louisiana State University Press, 1967).

At the head of general works useful for the study of recent southern politics stands V. O. Key, Jr.'s *Southern Politics in State and Nation* (New York: Knopf, 1949), the
classic survey of southern politics in the 1940s. Alfred O.
Hero, *The Southerner and World Affairs* (Baton Rouge:
Louisiana State University Press, 1965), is valuable to an
understanding of domestic politics because the author explored extensively the relationships of public opinion re-
garding both domestic and foreign affairs.

The most helpful accounts of general American politics
in recent decades have come from journalists and pundits.
Accounts of three presidential elections by Theodore H.
"Republicanism in North Carolina: John Motley More-
head's Campaign to Revive a Moribund Party, 1908–1910,"

White are essential references: *The Making of the President 1960, 1964* and *1968* (New York: Atheneum, 1961, 1965, 1969). On 1968 see also the report by three British newsmen: Lewis Chester, Godfrey Hodgson, and Bruce Page, *An American Melodrama: The Presidential Campaign of 1968* (New York: Viking, 1969). Among commentaries some of the most perceptive have come from Samuel Lubell: *The Future of American Politics* (New York: Harper, 1952); *Revolt of the Moderates* (New York: Harper, 1956); *White and Black: Test of a Nation* (New York: Harper & Row, 1964); and *The Hidden Crisis in American Politics* (New York: Norton, 1970).

The handbook for the southern strategy was Kevin P. Phillips, *The Emerging Republican Majority* (New Rochelle, N.Y.: Arlington House, 1969). Some of Phillips' assumptions are indirectly challenged in Richard M. Scammon and Ben J. Wattenberg, *The Real Majority* (New York: Coward-McAnn, 1970). Reg Murphy and Hal Gulliver, *The Southern Strategy* (New York: Scribners, 1971), is mainly an account of the 1970 elections. Frederick G. Dutton, *Changing Sources of Power: American Politics in the 1970s* (New York: McGraw-Hill, 1971), emphasizes the possibility of political fragmentation. A good introduction to the literature of party systems is William Nisbet Chambers and Walter Dean Burnham, eds., *The American Party Systems: Stages of Political Development* (New York: Oxford University Press, 1967), which includes essays by both historians and political scientists.

I. VARIATIONS ON A THEME BY HAYES

The pioneering studies of Republican southern strategies in the late nineteenth century are Vincent P. De Santis, *Republicans Face the Southern Question: The New De-*

parture Years, 1877–1897 (Baltimore: Johns Hopkins Press, 1959), and Stanley P. Hirshson, *Farewell to the Bloody Shirt: Northern Republicans and the Southern Negro, 1877–1893* (Bloomington: Indiana University Press, 1962). These excellent treatments cover much the same ground, but in a complementary rather than repetitious manner. De Santis focuses on southern developments and Hirshson on northern influences in making policy. An older work, Paul H. Buck, *The Road to Reunion, 1865–1900* (Boston: Little, Brown, 1937), includes two chapters on politics.

Detailed studies of southern strategies after the mid-1890s are almost nonexistent. One outstanding exception is Kenneth Wayne Dilda, "William Howard Taft and the Southern Policy of the Republican Party, 1906–1912" (M.A. thesis, East Carolina University, 1970), a thorough study which includes an exhaustive bibliography. See also, however, Henry F. Pringle, "Theodore Roosevelt and the South," *Virginia Quarterly Review*, IX (January 1933), 14–25; George E. Mowry, "The South and the Progressive Lily White Party of 1912," *Journal of American History*, XXVI (May 1940), 237–247; and Arthur S. Link, "Theodore Roosevelt and the South in 1912," *North Carolina Historical Review*, XXIII (1946), 313–324.

A model of what might be accomplished for other states is Olive Hall Shadgett, *The Republican Party in Georgia From Reconstruction through 1900* (Athens: University of Georgia Press, 1964). A briefer but praiseworthy treatment of a neighboring state is James W. Patton, "The Republican Party in South Carolina, 1876–1895," in Fletcher M. Green, ed., *Essays in Southern History* (Chapel Hill: University of North Carolina Press, 1949), pp. 91–111. On developments in North Carolina see three informative articles by Joseph F. Steelman: "Jonathan Elwood Cox and North Carolina in the Gubernatorial Campaign of 1908," *North Carolina Historical Review*, XLI (October 1964), 436–447;

ibid., xLII (April 1965), 153–168; and "Republican Party Strategists and the Issue of Fusion with Populists in North Carolina," ibid., xLVIII (July 1970), 244–269. Paul Casdorph, *A History of the Republican Party in Texas 1865–1965* (Austin: The Pemberton Press, 1965), offers mainly a detailed collectanea of facts.

Thomas B. Alexander has explored the subject of persistent Whiggery in a series of articles: "Whiggery and Reconstruction in Tennessee," *Journal of Southern History*, xVI (August 1950), 291–305; "Persistent Whiggery in Alabama and the Lower South, 1860–1867," *Alabama Review*, xII (January 1959), 35–52; "Persistent Whiggery in Mississippi: The Hinds County Gazette," *Journal of Mississippi History*, xXIII (April 1961), 71–93; and "Persistent Whiggery in the Confederate South, 1860–1877," *Journal of Southern History*, xxVII (August 1961), 305–329. Persistent Whiggery figures importantly in C. Vann Woodward's interpretation of the disputed election of 1876 in *Reunion and Reaction: The Compromise of 1877 and the End of Reconstruction* (Boston: Little, Brown, 1951).

The role of independent movements is examined in Charles Chilton Pearson, *The Readjuster Movement in Virginia* (New Haven: Yale University Press, 1917); Nelson Morehouse Blake, *William Mahone of Virginia: Soldier and Political Insurgent* (Richmond, Va.: Garrett & Massie, 1935) and two articles by Willie D. Halsell: "James R. Chalmers and 'Mahoneism' in Mississippi," *Journal of Southern History*, x (1944), 37–58; and "Republican Factionalism in Mississippi, 1882–1884," ibid., vII (February 1941), 84–101. The subject of political insurgency during the 1870s and 1880s is far from exhausted.

The agrarian revolt, which posed the greatest threat to the consolidation of the solid South, is the subject of an enormous literature. Among the best of many older state studies are Alex Mathews Arnett, *The Populist Movement in Georgia: A View of the "Agrarian Crusade" in the Light of Solid-South Politics* (New York: Columbia University Press, 1922), and Roscoe C. Martin, *The People's Party in Texas: A Study in Third Party Politics* (Austin: University of Texas, 1938). Three excellent new studies, all pertinent to the subject of southern strategies, are: Sheldon Hackney, *Populism to Progressivism in Alabama* (Princeton: Princeton University Press, 1969); William I. Hair, *Bourbonism and Agrarian Protest: Louisiana Politics, 1877–1900* (Baton Rouge: Louisiana State University Press, 1969); and William Warren Rogers, *The One-Gallused Rebellion: Agrarianism in Alabama, 1865–1896* (Baton Rouge: Louisiana State University Press, 1970). Among the biographical studies, C. Vann Woodward, *Tom Watson: Agrarian Rebel* (New York: Macmillan, 1938), is especially pertinent. On the fusion movement in North Carolina see Helen G. Edmonds, *The Negro and Fusion Politics in North Carolina, 1894–1901* (Chapel Hill: University of North Carolina Press, 1951).

II. THE DISRUPTION OF SOUTHERN DEMOCRACY

The development of sectional discontents in the Democratic party may be followed in David Burner, *The Politics of Provincialism: The Democratic Party in Transition, 1918–1932* (New York: Knopf, 1968); James T. Patterson iii, *Congressional Conservatism and the New Deal: The Growth of Conservative Coalition in Congress, 1933–1939* (Lexington: University of Kentucky Press, 1967); and Numan V. Bartley, *The Rise of Massive Resistance: Race and Politics during the 1950's* (Baton Rouge: Louisiana State University Press, 1969). The question of loyalty in the Democratic conventions of 1952, 1956, and 1960 is covered in

Abraham Holtzman, "Party Responsibility and Loyalty: New Rules in the Democratic Party," *Journal of Politics*, XXI (August 1960), 485–501; and Allan P. Sindler, "The Unsolid South: A Challenge to the Democratic National Party," in Alan F. Westin, ed., *The Uses of Power: 7 Cases in American Politics* (New York: Harcourt, Brace & World, 1962), pp. 229–283. Subsequent movements for reform in the nominating procedures are sketched in Alexander M. Bickel, *The New Age of Political Reform: The Electoral College, the Convention and the Party System* (New York: Harper & Row, 1968), pp. 29–34.

The best short treatment of the 1928 election in the South is in Key, *Southern Politics*, pp. 317–329. For Democratic politics in the country as a whole see Edmund A. Moore, *A Catholic Runs for President: The Campaign of 1928* (New York: Ronald, 1956). The most extensive treatment of Herbert Hoover's southern policies is in Lewinson, *Race, Class, & Party*, pp. 163–193. A perceptive contemporary analysis is H. C. Nixon, "The Changing Political Philosophy of the South," *Annals of the American Academy of Political and Social Science*, CLIII (January 1931), 246–250. On southern discontent with the New Deal see the works by Key and Lubell, previously cited; Frank Freidel, *F.D.R. and the South* (Baton Rouge: Louisiana State University Press, 1965); James T. Patterson III, "The Failure of Party Realignment in the South, 1937–1939," *Journal of Politics*, XXVII (August 1965), 602–617; and Jasper B. Shannon, "Presidential Politics in the South: 1938," *Journal of Politics*, I (May and August 1939), 146–170, 278–300. Shannon, *Toward a New Politics in the South* (Knoxville: University of Tennessee Press, 1949), includes his description of county-seat elites.

There is no definitive treatment of the Dixiecrat movement in print. A good brief account appears in Key, *Southern Politics*, pp. 329–344. But see also William G. Carleton,

"The Fate of Our Fourth Party," *Yale Review*, XXXVIII (Spring 1949), 449–459; Emile B. Ader, "Why the Dixiecrats Failed," *Journal of Politics*, xv (August 1953), 356–369; and Sarah McCulloh Lemmon, "The Ideology of the 'Dixiecrat' Movement," *Social Forces*, xxx (December 1951), 162–171. J. Harvie Wilkinson III, *Harry F. Byrd and the Changing Face of Virginia Politics, 1945–1966* (Charlottesville: University Press of Virginia, 1968), is a remarkably mature and felicitous account which originated as an undergraduate honors paper at Yale. An excellent state study oriented more toward political science is James R. Soukup, Clifton McClesky, and Harry Holloway, *Party and Factional Division in Texas* (Austin: University of Texas Press, 1964). There is nothing quite comparable for other states, but see also a briefer treatment which leans heavily on quantitative analysis: Numan V. Bartley, *From Thurmond to Wallace: Political Tendencies in Georgia 1948–1968* (Baltimore: Johns Hopkins Press, 1970).

Very useful for general coverage of recent events are several essays by Dewey W. Grantham, Jr.: "An American Politics for the South," in Charles G. Sellers, Jr., ed., *The Southerner as American* (Chapel Hill: University of North Carolina Press, 1960); "The South and the Reconstruction of American Politics," *Journal of American History*, LIII (September 1966), 227–246; and "The South and the Politics of Sectionalism," in Grantham, ed., *The South and the Sectional Image* (New York: Harper & Row, 1967), pp. 36–55. Two journalistic accounts of the more bizarre aspects of Southern politics are: Robert Sherrill, *Gothic Politics in the Deep South: Stars of the New Confederacy* (New York: Grossman, 1968), and Marshall Frady, *Wallace* (New York: World, 1968).

On the growing participation of blacks in southern politics see Andrew Buni, *The Negro in Virginia Politics 1902–*

1965 (Charlottesville: University Press of Virginia, 1967);
Donald R. Matthews and James W. Prothro, *Negroes and
the New Southern Politics* (New York: Harcourt, Brace &
World, 1966); and Pat Watters and Reece Cleghorn, *Climb-
ing Jacob's Ladder: The Arrival of Negroes in Southern
Politics* (New York: Harcourt, Brace & World, 1967).

III. TOWARD A PARTY SYSTEM

An essential point of departure for study of the emerging
Republicanism is G. Alexander Heard, *A Two-Party South?*
(Chapel Hill: University of North Carolina Press, 1952), a
far-sighted evaluation which appeared during a pivotal year
in southern politics. Fortunately an exhaustive account of
preconvention politics in that year is available: Paul T.
David, Malcolm Moos, and Ralph M. Goldman, *Presidential Nominating Politics in 1952* (5 vols., Baltimore: Johns
Hopkins Press, 1954). See especially Volume I, *The National Story*, and Volume III, *The South*.

Up to now, study of the new Republicanism has remained
the domain of political scientists, among whom the pioneer
is Donald S. Strong. His article, "The Presidential Election
in the South, 1952," *Journal of Politics*, XVII (August 1955),
343–389, initiated a study of the Eisenhower era which appeared in a slender volume—*Urban Republicanism in the
South* (University, Ala.: Bureau of Public Administration,
1960). See also Kenneth Vines, *Two Parties for Shreveport*
(New York: Holt, 1959), and Allan P. Sindler, ed., *Change
in the Contemporary South* (Durham: Duke University
Press, 1963), which includes essays by Strong, "Durable Republicanism in the South"; Philip E. Converse, "A Major
Political Realignment in the South?"; and Robert J.
Steamer, "Southern Disaffection with the National Demo-
cratic Party."

Bernard Cosman, formerly a student under Strong, has pursued the subject further in "Presidential Republicanism in the South, 1960," *Journal of Politics*, xxiv (May 1962), 303–322; *The Case of the Goldwater Delegates* (University, Ala.: Bureau of Public Administration, 1966); *Five States for Goldwater: Continuity and Change in Southern Voting Patterns* (University, Ala.: University of Alabama Press, 1966); and "Republicanism in the South: Goldwater's Impact Upon Voting Alignments in Congressional, Gubernatorial, and Senatorial Races," *Southwestern Social Science Quarterly*, xlviii (June 1967), 13–23. See also Bernard Cosman and Robert J. Huckshorn, eds., *Republican Politics: The 1964 Campaign and Its Aftermath for the Party* (New York: Praeger, 1968). Especially valuable articles dealing with developments in several states are Olive Hall Shadgett, "A History of the Republican Party in Georgia," *Georgia Review*, vii (Winter 1953), 428–442; Walter Dean Burnham, "The Alabama Senatorial Election of 1962: Return of Inter-Party Competition," *Journal of Politics*, xxvi (November 1964), 798–829; and Norman L. Parks, "Tennessee Politics Since Kefauver and Reece: A 'Generalist' View," ibid., xxviii (February 1966), 141–168.

Informative and critical reports on southern Republicanism appear in several studies sponsored by the liberal Republican Ripon Society: John G. Topping, Jr., John R. Lazarek, and William H. Linder, *Southern Republicanism and the New South* (Cambridge, Mass.: Republicans for Progress and the Ripon Society, 1966); Ripon Society, *The Lessons of Victory* (New York: Dial Press, 1969); and Michael S. Lottman, "The GOP and the South," in a special issue of *Ripon Forum*, vi (July–August 1970), 9–86. An analysis of the 1970 elections is Lottman, "The South: Southern Strategy Flops," *Ripon Forum*, vi (December 1970), 14–17, 24. Most issues of this periodical carry reports and comments on the South.

For developments in the Republican party during the 1960s, revolving largely around the Goldwater phenomenon, several journalistic accounts are useful: George F. Gilder and Bruce K. Chapman, *The Party that Lost Its Head* (New York: Knopf, 1966); Stephen Hess and David S. Broder, *The Republican Establishment: The Present and Future of the G.O.P.* (New York: Harper & Row, 1967); and Robert D. Novak, *The Agony of the G.O.P. 1964* (New York: Macmillan, 1965). F. Clifton White, with William J. Gill, *Suite 3505: The Story of the Draft Goldwater Movement* (New Rochelle, N.Y.: Arlington House, 1967), is a first-person account of the Goldwater movement; John H. Kessel, *The Goldwater Coalition: Republican Strategies in 1964*, is a political scientist's account.

Current magazines of news and commentary such as *Time, Newsweek, U.S. News, Nation, National Review* and *New Republic*, are useful for recent and continuing developments. Among the quarterly journals the following carry a number of pertinent articles: *American Political Science Review, Congressional Quarterly Weekly Report, Journal of Politics, New South, South Atlantic Quarterly, Southwestern Social Science Quarterly* and *Virginia Quarterly Review*.

Notes

ONE—*Variations on a Theme by Hayes*

1. *Les Guêpes*, new ed., 6 vols. (Paris: Michel Lévy, 1859–1863), VI, 305.

2. *The Anatomy of Revolution*, rev. ed. (New York: Vintage Books, [1952]).

3. Kevin P. Phillips, *The Emerging Republican Majority* (New Rochelle, N. Y.: Arlington House, 1969); Samuel Lubell, *The Hidden Crisis in American Politics* (New York: Norton, 1970); Richard M. Scammon and Ben J. Wattenberg, *The Real Majority* (New York: Coward-McCann, 1970); Reg Murphy and Hal Gulliver, *The Southern Strategy* (New York: Scribners, 1971); Frederick G. Dutton, *Changing Sources of Power: American Politics in the 1970s* (New York: McGraw-Hill, 1971).

4. Phillips, *Emerging Republican Majority*, p. 461.

5. Nelson W. Polsby, "An Emerging Republican Majority?" *The Public Interest*, number 17 (Fall 1969), p. 119.

6. See especially Thomas B. Alexander, "Persistent Whiggery in the Confederate South, 1860–1877," *Journal of Southern History*, XXVII (1961), 305–329.

7. Raymond (Miss.) *Hinds County Gazette*, October 21, 1868, quoted in Thomas B. Alexander, ed., "Persistent Whiggery in Mississippi: The Hinds County Gazette," *Journal of Mississippi History*, XXIII (1961), 76.

8. See C. Vann Woodward, *Reunion and Reaction: The Compromise of 1877 and the End of Reconstruction* (Boston: Little, Brown, 1951).

9. Rutherford B. Hayes to James G. Blaine, September 14, 1876, quoted in Gail Hamilton, *Biography of James G. Blaine* (Norwich, Conn.: Henry Bill, 1895), p. 422.

10. Quoted in *Letters of Mr. William E. Chandler Relative to the So-Called Southern Policy of President Hayes* (Concord, N.H.: Monitor and Statesman, 1878), p. 8.

11. For detailed treatments of the policies of Hayes and his successors to the 1890s, see Vincent P. De Santis, *Republicans Face the Southern Question—The New Departure Years, 1877–1897* (Baltimore: Johns Hopkins Univ. Press, 1959), and Stanley P. Hirshson, *Farewell to the Bloody Shirt: Northern Republicans & the Southern Negro, 1877–1893* (Bloomington: Indiana Univ. Press, 1962).

12. Quoted in Hirshson, *Farewell to the Bloody Shirt*, p. 39.

13. *Hayes: The Diary of a President, 1875–1881*, ed. T. Harry Williams (New York: McKay, 1964), p. 164.

14. William Lloyd Garrison to William E. Chandler, January 21, 1878, in *Letters of Mr. William E. Chandler Relative to the So-Called Southern Policy of President Hayes*, p. 42.

15. *Hayes: The Diary of a President*, p. 169; Hayes quoted in Hirshson, p. 49.

16. Quoted in C. Vann Woodward, *Origins of the New South, 1877–1913* (Baton Rouge: Louisiana State University Press, 1951), p. 49.

17. Quoted in Hirshson, *Farewell to the Bloody Shirt*, p. 107.

18. *Atlanta Constitution*, October 10, 1892, quoted in Olive Hall Shadgett, *The Republican Party in Georgia from Reconstruction through 1900* (Athens: University of Georgia Press, 1964), p. 150.

19. Hilary A. Herbert, ed., *Why the Solid South? or, Reconstruction and its Results* (Baltimore: R. H. Woodward, 1890).

20. Alex M. Arnett, *The Populist Movement in Georgia: A View of the "Agrarian Crusade" in the Light of Solid-South Politics* (New York: Columbia University, 1922), p. 184.

21. Herbert Croly, *Marcus Alonzo Hanna: His Life and Work* (New York: Macmillan, 1923), pp. 175–176; Shadgett, *Republican Party in Georgia*, pp. 122–151; quotation from Charles S. Olcott, *The Life of William McKinley*, 2 vols. (Boston: Houghton Mifflin, 1916), I, 226–227.

22. Theodore Roosevelt to Henry Cabot Lodge, October 11, [1901], quoted in Henry F. Pringle, *Theodore Roosevelt: A Biography* (New York: Harcourt, Brace, 1931), p. 247. See also pp. 8, 230, 248, and Pringle, "Theodore Roosevelt and the South," *Virginia Quarterly Review*, IX (1933), 14–25.

23. Woodward, *Origins of the New South*, p. 463. See also pp. 463–467 and George E. Mowry, "The South and the Progressive Lily White Party of 1912," *Journal of Southern History*, VI (1940), 237–247.

24. Kenneth Wayne Dilda, "William Howard Taft and the Southern Policy of the Republican Party, 1906–1912," M.A. thesis, East Carolina University, 1970.

25. Andrew Sinclair, *The Available Man: The Life Behind the Masks of Warren Gamaliel Harding* (New York: Macmillan, 1965), pp. 230–235; Robert K. Murray, *The Harding Era: Warren G. Harding and His Administration* (Minneapolis: Univ. of Minnesota Press, 1969), pp. 397–403; quotation from *New York Times*, October 27, 1921.

26. Donald R. McCoy, *Calvin Coolidge: The Quiet President* (New York: Macmillan, 1966), 328–329.

TWO—*The Disruption of Southern Democracy*

1. Burr J. Ramage, "The Dissolution of the 'Solid South,'" *Sewanee Review*, IV (1896), 493.

2. Watterson in Hirshson, *Farewell to the Bloody Shirt* (Bloomington: Indiana Univ. Press, 1962); Beverly in C. Vann Woodward, *Origins of the New South, 1877–1913* (Baton Rouge: Louisiana State University Press, 1951), p. 243; Walter Hines Page, "The Solid South," in William Howard Taft, *The South and the National Government* (pamphlet, n.p., n.d.), p. 6; Enoch M. Banks, "The Passing of the Solid South," *South Atlantic Quarterly*, VIII (1909), 101–106; James W. Garner, "New Politics for the South," *Annals of the American Academy of Political and Social Science*, XXXV (1910), 172–183. Many other examples are cited in the bibliography of Dilda, "William Howard Taft and the Southern Policy of the Republican Party, 1906–1912."

3. Freeman in Edwin Mims, *The Advancing South: Stories of Progress and Reaction* (Garden City: Doubleday, Page, 1926), p. 193. For a summary of arguments against the one-party system see Vladimir O. Key, Jr., *Southern Politics in State and Nation* (New York: Knopf, 1949), pp. 302–311.

4. On the political discontents of the 1920s as they affected the Democratic party see David Burner, *The Politics of Provincialism: The Democratic Party in Transition, 1918–1932* (New York: Knopf, 1968).

5. Wilbur J. Cash, "Jehovah of the Tar Heels," *American Mercury*, XVII (1929), 318. For a summary of the 1928 election in the South see Key, *Southern Politics*, pp. 318–329.

6. T. J. Wertenbaker, "Up from the Depths," *Princeton Alumni Weekly*, XXIX (1928–1929), 453.

7. Hoover statement, March 26, 1929, quoted in Monroe N. Work, ed., *Negro Year Book*, 1931–1932 (Tuskegee Institute, Ala.: Negro Year Book Publishing Co., 1931), p. 93; Paul Lewinson, *Race, Class, & Party: A History of Negro Suffrage and White Politics in the South* (London and New York: Oxford University Press, 1932), pp. 166–185.

8. W. J. Cash, *The Mind of the South* (New York: Knopf, 1941), pp. 420–421.

9. Jasper B. Shannon, *Toward a New Politics in the South* (Knoxville: University of Tennessee Press, 1949), p. 44; Ralph McGill, *The South and the Southerner* (Boston: Atlantic-Little, Brown, 1964), pp. 161–164.

10. Harry S. Ashmore, *An Epitaph for Dixie* (New York: Norton, 1958), pp. 100–101.

11. Alexander Heard, *A Two-Party South?* (Chapel Hill: University of North Carolina Press, 1952), pp. 158, 257–258.

12. *Congressional Record*, 75 Cong., 1 Sess., Appendix, p. 661.

13. Heard, *A Two-Party South?*, pp. 158–159.

14. Lucy Randolph Mason to Eleanor Roosevelt, February 11, 1938, in Mason Papers (Manuscripts Division, Duke University Library, Durham, N.C.).

15. *A Senate Journal, 1943–1945* (New York: McGraw-Hill, 1963), p. 138.

16. Key, *Southern Politics*, pp. 329–344; Numan V. Bartley, *The Rise of Massive Resistance: Race and Politics in the South During the 1950's* (Baton Rouge: Louisiana State University Press, 1969), pp. 32–37; Humphrey in *New York Times*, July 15, 1948.

17. Bartley, *The Rise of Massive Resistance*, p. 32.

18. The issue of loyalty in the Democratic conventions of 1952, 1956, and 1960 is treated in Allan P. Sindler, "The Unsolid South: A Challenge to the Democratic National Party," in Alan F. Westin, ed., *The Uses of Power: 7 Cases in American Politics* (New York: Harcourt, Brace & World, 1962), pp. 229–283. See also Paul T. David et al., *Presidential Nominating Politics in 1952*, 5 vols. (Baltimore: Johns Hopkins Press, 1954), i, 103–127.

19. Bartley, *The Rise of Massive Resistance*, pp. 108–125.

20. Sindler, "The Unsolid South," pp. 268–272.

21. Ibid., pp. 163–168.

22. James A. Michener, *Report of the County Chairman* (New York: Random House, 1961), p. 186.

23. For a summary of reforms in the 1964 and 1968 conventions see Alexander M. Bickel, *The New Age of Political Reform: The Electoral College, the Convention and the Party System* (New York: Harper & Row, 1968), pp. 29–34.

24. *The Presidential Nominating Conventions 1968* (Washington: Congressional Quarterly Service, 1968), passim.

25. Robert C. Sherrill, "The GOP in the South," *Nation*, ccvii (August 5, 1968), 76.

26. *New York Times*, March 15, 1971.

27. Ibid., August 30, 1970; *Time*, May 31, 1971, p. 14.

28. Ibid., January 24, 1971, iv, 10: 1–2.

29. William G. Carleton, "Two-Party South?" *Virginia Quarterly Review*, xli (1965), 489.

THREE—*Toward a Party System*

1. Virginius Dabney, "What the GOP Is Doing in the South," *Atlantic*, ccxxvi (May, 1963), 87; Blease in *Congressional Record*, 69 Cong., 2 Sess., p. 5362.

2. Alexander Heard, *A Two-Party South?* (Chapel Hill: University of North Carolina Press, 1952), p. 37.

3. V. O. Key, Jr., *Southern Politics in State and Nation* (New York: Knopf, 1949), p. 220. For a discussion of southern Republican types see Heard, *A Two-Party South?*, pp. 37–53.

4. Ibid., pp. 292–297.

5. *New York Times*, February 2, 1961. Obituary of Perry Howard.

6. The details may be followed in Paul T. David et al., *Presidential Nominating Politics in 1952* (4 vols., Baltimore: The Johns Hopkins Press, 1954), Vol. i, *The National Story*, and Vol. iii, *The South*. See also Paul Casdorph, *A History of the Republican Party in Texas 1865–1965* (Austin, Tex.: The Pemberton Press, 1965), pp. 172–197, and Olive Hall Shadgett, "A History of the Republican Party in Georgia," *Georgia Review*, vii (1953), 440–441.

7. *New York Times*, September 23, October 1, 1952; Harry Golden, *Mr. Kennedy and the Negroes* (Cleveland and New York: World, 1964), p. 15. Golden's eyewitness account of the Columbia meeting was called to my attention by the late Professor Joseph L. Morrison.

8. For analysis of the 1952 election see Donald S. Strong, "The Presidential Election in the South, 1952," *Journal of Politics*, xvii (August 1955) 343–389. See also Strong's *Urban Republicanism in the South* (University, Alabama: Bureau of Public Administration, 1960) and his "Durable Republicanism in the South," in Allan P. Sindler, ed., *Change in the Contemporary South* (Durham, N. C.: Duke Univ. Press, 1963), pp. 174–194.

9. Strong, *Urban Republicanism in the South* and "Durable Republicanism in the South."

10. Stephen Hess and David S. Broder, *The Republican Establishment: The Present and Future of the G. O. P.* (New York: Harper & Row, 1967), p. 336.

11. Theodore H. White, *The Making of the President 1960* (New York: Atheneum, 1961), pp. 304–308.

12. Strong, "Durable Republicanism in the South," pp. 185–186; Bernard Cosman, "Presidential Republicanism in the South, 1960," *Journal of Politics*, xxiv (May 1962), 303–322.

13. Strong, "The Presidential Election in the South, 1952," p. 382.

14. Francis Pickens Miller, "The Democratic Party in the South: Signs of Restiveness," *Christianity and Crisis*, xxi (May 1, 1961), 63–64.

15. *U. S. News & World Report*, liii (October 22, 1962), 61; James R. Soukup, Clifton McClesky, and Harry Holloway, *Party and Factional Division in Texas* (Austin: University of Texas Press, 1964), 43–44, 61.

16. Sindler, "The Unsolid South," p. 242.

17. Strong, "Durable Republicanism in the South," pp. 183–184.

18. *New York Times*, June 9, 11, 1957, November 26, 1962, January 22, 1964; "Rip Van Dixie," London *Economist*, clxxxix (November 29, 1958), 323–324; "C. Q. Fact Sheet on Southern Republicanism," *Congressional Quarterly Weekly Report*, xxi (January 11, 1963), 37–41; John H. Kessel, *The Goldwater Coalition: Republican Strategies in 1964* (Indianapolis: Bobbs-Merrill, 1968), pp. 39–40.

19. Hess and Broder, *The Republican Establishment*, p. 340.

20. Strong, "Durable Republicanism in the South," pp. 188–189; Walter Dean Burnham, "The Alabama Senatorial Election of 1962: Return of Inter-Party Competition," *Journal of Politics*, xxvi (November 1964), 798–829; John C. Topping, Jr., John R. Lazarek, and William H. Linder, *Southern Republicanism and the New South* (Cambridge, Mass.: privately printed, 1966), p. 75.

21. F. Clifton White, with William J. Gill, *Suite 3505: The Story of the Draft Goldwater Movement* (New Rochelle, N.Y.: Arlington House, 1967), pp. 19–24. White, passim, is the source for the following account except where otherwise indicated.

22. William A. Rusher, "Crossroads for the GOP," *National Review*, xiv (February 12, 1963), 109–112. See also Ralph De Toledano, *The Win-*

ning Side: The Case for Goldwater Republicanism (New York: Putnam, 1963).

23. Eric F. Goldman, *The Tragedy of Lyndon Johnson* (New York: Knopf, 1969).

24. Hess and Broder, *The Republican Establishment*, pp. 335–336; George F. Gilder and Bruce K. Chapman, *The Party that Lost Its Head* (New York: Knopf, 1966), p. 62.

25. Theodore H. White, *The Making of the President, 1964* (New York: Atheneum, 1965), p. 136; Robert D. Novak, *The Agony of the G.O.P., 1964* (New York: Macmillan, 1965), p. 177.

26. *New South*, xxi (Spring 1966), 91; Richard Rovere, "The Campaign: Goldwater," *New Yorker*, xl (October 1964), 208–211.

27. For analyses of the Goldwater campaign and vote see Bernard Cosman, *The Case of the Goldwater Delegates* (University, Ala.: Bureau of Public Administration, 1966) and *Five States for Goldwater: Continuity and Change in Southern Voting Patterns* (University, Ala.: Univ. of Alabama Press, 1966).

28. Rusher, "Crossroads for the GOP," p. 112.

29. William G. Carleton, "Two-Party South?" *Virginia Quarterly Review*, xli (1965), 490.

30. Richard M. Scammon, ed., *America Votes: A Handbook of Contemporary American Election Statistics* (New York: Macmillan, 1956–1960), Vols. 1–7, passim.

31. *Congressional Quarterly Weekly Report*, xxiii (January 1, 1965), 14; J. Harvie Wilkinson iii, *Harry Byrd and the Changing Face of Virginia Politics, 1945–1966* (Charlottesville: Univ. Press of Virginia, 1968), pp. 228–229.

32. Hess and Broder, *The Republican Establishment*, pp. 340–342.

33. Robert Sherrill, "The GOP in the South," *Nation*, ccvii (August 5, 1968), 75.

34. Ibid., p. 77.

35. Lewis Chester, Godfrey Hodgson, and Bruce Page, *An American Melodrama: The Presidential Campaign of 1968* (New York: Dell, 1969), pp. 489–497.

36. Ibid., 498–500, 532–538; White, *The Making of the President 1968* (New York: Atheneum, 1969), pp. 171–172, 279.

37. Hess and Broder, *The Republican Establishment*, p. 180.

38. Michael S. Lottman, "The South: Southern Strategy Flops," *Ripon Forum*, vi (December 1970), 70.

39. Topping, et al., *Southern Republicanism and the New South*, p. 92.

40. *Wall Street Journal*, October 4, 1963.

41. Richard Hofstadter, *The Idea of a Party System: The Rise of Legitimate Opposition in the United States, 1780–1840* (Berkeley: Univ. of California Press, 1969).

Index

Browning, Gordon, 38
Brownsville, Texas, 18
Bryan, William Jennings, 16, 19, 23, 26, 30
Busing, 68, 69
Byrd, Harry F., 34, 39, 41, 42, 66
Byrnes, James F., 39, 51

Carleton, William G., 65
Carpetbaggers, 7, 15, 49
Carswell, G. Harrold, 70
Carter, Jimmy, 44
Cash, Wilbur, J., 29
Catholic issue, 27
Chandler, William E., 11
Chapel Hill regionalists, 29
Charleston, South Carolina, 27, 42
Charlotte, North Carolina, 69
Chattanooga, Tennessee, 27
Citizens' councils, 41
Civil rights, 2, 35, 36, 42, 44, 54, 59
Civil Rights Act of 1964, 63
Civil War, 28
Civil War Centennial, 1
Clay, Henry, 6
Cleveland, Grover, 5, 14, 23
Columbia, South Carolina, 51
Compromise of 1877, 8, 33, 38
Conkling, Roscoe, 11
"Conservative chic," 52
Conservatives, 7, 32; conservative coalition, 34
"Constitutional Democrats of Texas," 32
Constitutional Union party, 6
Coolidge, Calvin, 20, 47
Cosman, Bernard, 64
County-seat elites, 30
Creager, R. B., 50
Crum, William D., 18
Currency issue, 19

Daily Worker, 51
Dallas, Texas, 27, 62

DATE DUE

DATE DUE			
OCT 12 '76			
OCT 26 '76			
NO 9 '77			
NO 22 '77			
DE 13 '78			
OC 24 '80			
RD			PRINTED IN U.S.A